Business Admin Student Guide
NVQ Level 3

CW01067583

Chris Ager

Stanley Thornes (Publishers) Ltd

First published in 1992 by:
Stanley Thornes (Publishers) Ltd
Ellenborough House
Wellington Street
CHELTENHAM GL50 1YD
England

Reprinted 1993
Reprinted 1994

A catalogue record for this book is available from the British Library.

ISBN 0–7487–1399–9

Typeset by Tech-Set, Gateshead, Tyne & Wear.
Printed and bound in Great Britain at Redwood Books, Trowbridge, Wiltshire.

Contents

Introduction

To gain a National Vocational Qualification (NVQ) Award in Administration you must be able to perform practical tasks successfully.

The activities in this book follow the format of the NCVQ Administration Level 3 Units and Elements.

To obtain a full NVQ Administration Level 3 Award you will need to achieve competence in the ten main Units. If you do not achieve competence in all Units the appropriate examining body would award a Unit Certificate stating the Units in which you have been successful. Whenever possible the performance of a task should be carried out in an office environment using up-to-date equipment.

To ensure you are properly assessed for your achievements you will need to be attached to an approved Training Centre and to register with one of the appropriate Examining Bodies approved to run NVQ Administration Level 3, for example, the London Chamber of Commerce or Royal Society of Arts.

Once your Assessors have agreed that you have achieved competence in particular Unit(s) and your Competence Transcript has been prepared then it will require the verification of the Examining Board's Representative before the Award is given.

This book is an aid to students to develop the underpinning knowledge required in the Units and to enable them to gain practical experience towards achieving competence. It is also intended to provide some of the structural work required for the Award. The student discovery learning aspect within the various activities should provide the remaining part.

This book alone will not enable the user to be assessed as fully competent.

Acknowledgements

I would like to express my thanks to the following organisations and companies for their help in compiling this book:

British Rail, British Telecom, Canon (UK) Ltd, Lloyds Bank PLC, Mercury Communications Ltd, Pitney Bowes PLC and The West Midlands Fire Service.

I would also like to thank my husband Mike for his help and support.

Communication systems

Main elements covered

1.1 Organise allocation and despatch of mail
1.2 Use the telephone system to the full
1.3 Transmit and receive information using electronic equipment

Supplementary elements covered

2.2 Locate and abstract information from unspecified sources
2.3 Organise and present information in a variety of formats
5.1 Produce text from oral and written material using an alphanumeric keyboard
10.1 Monitor and maintain health and safety within the work area

Element 1.1 – Organise allocation and despatch of mail

Mail is a very important part of the communication system in any company. Although there are many electronic methods of communication now in operation the mail still has a role to play in ensuring a relatively cheap mode of contacting businesses and individuals almost anywhere in the world.

One of the main features of an efficient mail service in a company is that mail should be opened and distributed immediately on arrival at the organisation. Some firms prefer the use of a private Post Office box which enables them to collect their post at convenient times.

In many companies much of the post is just addressed to the organisation. Some companies state that all correspondence should be addressed to a named person or post-holder, for example, the chief executive or managing director. In other cases most incoming mail may be addressed to named individual employees.

There is usually a person (or persons) who is nominated to deal with the post. This individual is frequently asked to start work earlier than the rest of the staff with time off later in the day to compensate. Such an arrangement means that those coming into the office later find their mail ready for them on their desks when they arrive.

Activity 1.1.1

You work in a firm of solicitors. There have been many complaints recently about the late arrival of the morning mail to the firm and about the time it takes to distribute that mail to individual staff. Your supervisor has asked you to investigate the situation and see if you have any recommendations which might remedy the problem.

Set out your findings in a brief memo to your supervisor.

Post room equipment

There is a wide range of equipment manufactured specifically for speeding and streamlining the allocation and despatch of mail. Letter openers, date stamps, folding machines, electronic franking machines, electronic scales and such items as pigeon-holes and trolleys, are some of the aids to speed up this service. Addressing machines have now largely been superseded by high-speed computerised labelling programs and equipment.

Modern postal scales and franking machines incorporate electronic technology to provide a system which gives you the facility to:

- Place the item on the postal scale and at the touch of a button the exact postage required is set automatically on the postage meter.

- Use colour-coded keys which give an instant read-out on additional postal fees required for such items as Special Delivery, Registered Mail, Swiftair and Datapost.

Electronic scales and franking machine

Another useful facility that may be available in a modern post room is the 'Postage by Phone' service. Whilst some franking machines require the user to buy credit cards from the Post Office modern electronic technology now enables you to:

1 Pick up the memory phone attached to your Postage by Phone meter and call the Postage by Phone Data Centre.

2 Answer security check questions.
3 Listen to the computerised voice for your unique postage resetting code.
4 Enter the code into your postage meter.
5 Reset the meter to the appropriate amount of credit.

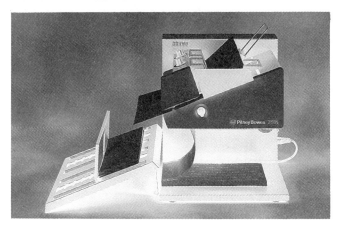

Automatic labeller

If your company has a large amount of outgoing mail to be prepared and posted it may be worth considering purchasing a system which uses modern microtechnology to automate the system, as shown on page 4. The operator is in charge of the system via the use of the touch-sensitive screen.

It should be remembered that post room procedures will vary from company to company depending on type and size of the organisation.

FACT FINDER

Basic procedure for incoming mail

Always be aware that there may be unusual items in the mail, some perfectly harmless, some potentially dangerous (see 'Health, safety and security procedures when handling mail' on pages 6–7).

1 When receiving and signing for items of mail for the company check to ensure that they are what they are said to be and that they are not damaged in any way.

If they are damaged there may be a Post Office label to this effect. If not, point the damage out to the delivery person. Procedures then need to be put into effect to claim compensation for damage.

2 Initially, all the envelopes should be turned the same way round.

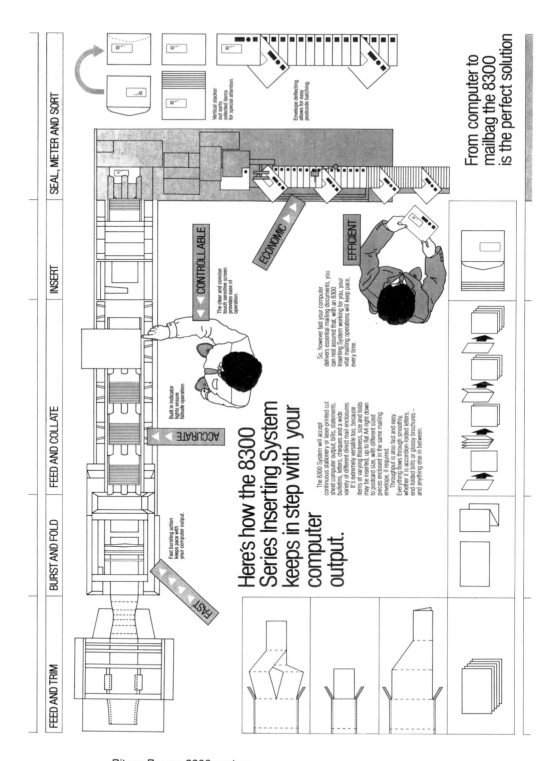

Pitney Bowes 8300 system

3 A sort is then carried out:

a) Any mail marked urgent is immediately dealt with as appropriate.
b) Private, personal and confidential mail is removed from the main bundle.
c) Items addressed to specific individuals are put to one side.
d) The remaining mail is opened, checking that any stated enclosures are present. If enclosures are missing a note should be made to this effect on the communication and a follow-up action put into effect.

The decision as to who is to receive the mail should be taken by someone with a good knowledge of the company and its various functions.

4 Mail is date stamped, taking care not to obliterate any important text.

5 Remittances received in the post are generally entered in a remittances book and passed to the cashier.

6 Circulation slips are prepared for items requiring the attention of more than one member of staff. If appropriate, a photocopy may be made for each person.

7 Distribute the mail as soon as possible.

Companies often keep used envelopes, initially in case there is any query over the mail, and subsequently, as an economy measure, for internal mail.

Activity 1.1.2

Referring to the incoming mail procedure set out above or to the one which is used at your place of employment, state the role the supervisor would take and the task(s) s/he would perform.

Set out your suggestions on an information sheet entitled 'The duties of the supervisor – incoming mail'.

Basic outgoing mail procedure

As with incoming mail this procedure may vary considerably from company to company.

In some large companies with a central mail facility a special collection service is in operation with collection points throughout the building and with collection times known to all staff.

As an administrative assistant you may be responsible for monitoring the procedures for outgoing mail. Staff should check that all enclosures are present, that the communication has been signed by the appropriate executive, and that the letter and address on the envelope correspond.

In the post room first and second class post is bundled separately to aid its journey through the mail system. The mail would be weighed and the necessary postage affixed either with an ordinary postage stamp or by using a franking machine. Documentation for any special postal services required (for example, Recorded Delivery or Registered Post) is prepared.

Mail may be collected from the company's premises by special arrangement or taken to the Post Office. Franked mail should not be posted in an ordinary post box.

With all mail handling procedures great care should be exercised to ensure that good safety and security practices are followed at all times.

FACT FINDER

Health, safety and security procedures when handling mail

1 Always be aware that an item may contain dangerous substances.

   If you are at all suspicious about a piece of mail then do not open it or press or prod it in any way – leave well alone. Leave the office, lock the door and inform your security officer immediately.

   Treat as suspicious any item which:

   has an unusual smell;
   has any liquid seeping from it;
   has unusual wrapping;
   is of unusual size, weight or shape;
   has strange writing or spelling on the packet;
   has protruding wires.

2 Always check that any item being sent in the mail service is one which is allowed. Never send such items as aerosols or lighters.

3 Always ensure that items are well packed with secure fastening. There are a number of different packing materials to use, such as Bubble Sheets and Jiffy Bags, that ensure items are safe and secure.

4 Always ensure that items are correctly and clearly labelled. Use HANDLE WITH CARE, FRAGILE and PHOTOGRAPHS - DO NOT BEND labels when appropriate.

5 Ensure that all customs labels are completed clearly and correctly.

6 Ensure that the correct service is being used, for example, the Registered Post service for cash, otherwise you may find there is inadequate or no compensation at all for any losses incurred.

If you are supervising the mail ensure that all staff are fully aware of these procedures.

Activity 1.1.3

As the mail room supervisor you are concerned that staff are paying insufficient attention to health, safety and security matters when dealing with mail. Compose a memo to the staff explaining the need for them to be on a constant lookout for suspicious packages and to follow good health and safety procedures at all times.

FACT FINDER

Range of postal services

There is a wide range of services available to the postal user. Leaflets on these services may be obtained from your local Post Office. Services include:

Cash on delivery　This service allows for cash to be collected from the addressee on delivery of a package.

Certificate of posting　This may be obtained for inland ordinary letters and parcels, and overseas ordinary letters. It gives the sender proof of posting and compensation for loss or damage provided all the required conditions have been met. There is no compensation if money or jewellery is sent in the ordinary post.

Royal Mail Special Delivery (RMSD)　This service offers the user extra assurance that their important letters or packets will arrive the next working day after posting. There is a fee for this service in addition to first class postage.

Recorded Delivery　This service provides the user with a Certificate of Posting and a signature on delivery. This service is especially suitable for sending important documents through the post. Compensation is payable for loss or damage, although not for money or jewellery. There is a fee for this service plus first or second class postage.

Registered Post　This service provides the user with a Certificate of Posting and a signature on delivery. It is especially suitable for sending valuables through the post. Compensation is payable for loss or damage depending on the level paid for. There is a fee for this service plus first class postage.

DataPost   This service provides same day collection and delivery between most UK business centres. If an item fails to be delivered on time the full fee may be reclaimed from the Post Office. Insurance cover included in the fee provides compensation should an item be lost or damaged. An express service is available internationally (see below). If use of Datapost is likely to be regular, contracts may be arranged.

Business Reply Service   A licence from the Post Office is required to operate this pre-paid postal service. It is appropriate in situations where the licensees wish to encourage people to contact them without having the expense of postage. Special stationery has to be prepared and approved by the Post Office. The envelopes are distinguished by the large 1 (first class) and 2 (second class) numbers, and thick, black parallel lines printed on them. Also available as an international service.

FreePost   A licence is also required to operate a FreePost Service. This is a pre-paid service which does not require special stationery unless it is to be sent first class. When being used under the second class postage the user adds the word FREEPOST to the address.

Activity 1.1.4

You are working for a small mail order firm. Your supervisor is concerned that appropriate postal services are not being used by the company.

1 To remedy this situation you have been asked to provide guidelines to help staff when deciding which postal service would be most appropriate and to give comparative costs. Set out your findings on a fact sheet to be distributed to staff.

2 In addition, you have been asked to find out about the use of the Postage Forward and Trakback Parcels services. It is thought they may be useful services for the company to use. What do you think? Set out your information in a memo to your supervisor.

Overseas mail

Extra care should be taken when sending items abroad through the postal service. Always check that the receiving country allows the item to be imported. Letters and packets are liable to be opened for examination by customs overseas and the contents should be declared on special forms.

As with all post, take care with labelling. Make sure you use the appropriate labels, for example, blue Airmail labels or red Swiftair labels.

If you are sending printed papers overseas make sure that they may be easily opened for examination by customs and easily repacked.

International mail delivery services

These services include:

Aerogrammes which are the easiest and cheapest method of international correspondence. The same cost applies to all destinations.

International registration which is a similar service to the inland Recorded Delivery service. There is a fee in addition to the postage charge.

Swiftair which is a priority letter service. Whilst Swiftair items travel with the ordinary airmail service they receive priority handling and express sorting treatment. There is a fee for this service in addition to the postage. Special Swiftpacks may be bought from a Post Office.

An **insurance service** which is available for high-value items up to a limit of £1500. This is available with both letter and parcel post.

International Datapost which offers an express, guaranteed delivery service to over 160 countries and territories world-wide. As with the UK Datapost, should your item fail to arrive by the agreed time, you may claim a full refund. The fee includes insurance cover for loss or damage, and consequential loss.

Activity 1.1.5

Your employer wishes to send some magazines through the post to places in Europe and Asia. This is to be on a regular basis. S/he has asked you to investigate the most appropriate service to use for this item and to find out as much detailed information on recommendations for packing, cost, weight limit, delivery time and any other specific instructions associated with the service.

S/he has also asked you to investigate delivery or courier agencies, other than the Post Office, available to you locally. Give company names and addresses, and any other information you can obtain, such as distances carried, time factors and costs.

Set out your findings on two separate information sheets.

Element 1.2 – Use the telephone service to the full

Whatever the size of a business it will almost certainly have a telephone facility. External services may vary from a single line with one telephone number to a sophisticated system involving the employment of several switchboard operators. Direct private lines may also be installed to connect various buildings on the same site.

In order for the company to run as effectively as possible it is important that switchboard operators and all those using the telephone system should have a full and up-to-date knowledge of the company's structure and its operations.

Activity 1.2.1

1　Investigate the company structure of either your place of work or where you are studying. Produce an information sheet showing the key members of staff and their functions (if you have not already prepared such a sheet for Unit 3).

2　Find out what products or services your company or study centre provides and add them to the information sheet you have prepared in 1 above.

One of the most common tasks for anyone working in an office is making and receiving telephone calls. The telephone is frequently a first contact point for many new customers and the care with which telephone calls are made and received should reflect this fact.

It is also important to answer other people's phone calls and to take a message if necessary. If you are out of the office for any length of time you should consider diverting your calls to a business colleague.

Activity 1.2.2

What makes a good telephone user?

Your company wishes to employ a new clerk in the sales office. One of their most important duties will be contacting both present and potential customers and dealing with complaints.

What specific qualities would you expect from an applicant for such a post? Write out your points clearly so that they may be incorporated into the information sent out to those applying for the post.

FACT
FINDER

Making a telephone call

1 Always be aware of the high cost of long distance calls and the different charge times. (Some firms stipulate that non-emergency, long-distance calls should only be made after 1.00 pm which is a cheaper charge time.)

2 Plan the call by always preparing well before making the call. Make sure you know exactly why you are making the call and have the necessary file containing all the essential facts in front of you.

3 Know the correct name and title of the person you wish to contact and, if possible, a named substitute.

4 Identify yourself and the organisation you are representing.

5 If you are disconnected, having initiated the call, it is accepted practice that you will re-call the number.

6 Always confirm in writing any arrangements made over the telephone.

7 It is bad practice to divulge confidential information over the telephone.

Activity 1.2.3

The junior in your office is shy and worried about making and receiving telphone calls. You decide you will help her/him by setting out the correct procedure to follow. Write down your comments on a fact sheet which would be useful to any member of staff with a similar problem.

Emergency procedures

Always sound friendly and helpful when receiving a telephone call and be sure to identify yourself. Should you ever receive a call stating that a bomb has been planted on the premises then you should attempt to keep your caller on the line and to find out as much information as possible. At the very least try to find out:

- The location of the bomb.
- The time it is expected to explode.
- The identification of the caller.

Write down as many details as you can. Inform your security officer and the police immediately.

FACT FINDER

Standard telephone service summary – inland and international

Operator Services – for inland dial 100; for international dial 155.

Directory Enquiries – for inland calls dial 192; for international calls dial 153.

International Direct Dialling (IDD) – it is possible to phone many countries in the world without going through the operator. The format of such numbers is as follows:

International code – country code – area code – local number.

Alarm calls – you may arrange to be 'called up' by the operator at any time, for a small charge.

Personal calls – you may make a personal call through the operator naming a specific person to whom you wish to speak. If that person is not available there is usually no charge for the call. This service is available on inland and international calls.

Advice of duration and charge – it is possible to place a call through the operator and ask for this service. When the call has been completed the operator will phone the user with the cost of the call. This service is available on inland and international calls.

Telephone credit card calls – inland telephone calls may be made and charged to credit cards. However, with international calls these cards may only be used to call the country in which the cards were issued.

Call collect service – you may use this service both for inland and international calls. The connection is made through the operator with the caller paying the call charge, providing of course that they agree.

UK direct – this service is for incoming international calls and is available only from certain countries. It enables you to get access to an English-speaking operator in the UK who will accept your British Telecom credit card or arrange a collect call.

Facsimile – for British Telecom's facsimile service the sender dials 150 (see also Element 1.3 later). The sender is able to dictate a fax to be sent anywhere in the UK and to most other countries.

Although British Telecom has had a monopoly in providing a range of telephone services in the UK, Mercury Communications and other companies are increasingly providing similar services.

Activity 1.2.4

Your employer has heard that Mercury Communications offer a cheaper service than British Telecom and s/he has asked you to investigate the situation. Find out whether there are any advantages to a company to change from British Telecom to Mercury Communications.

Set out your findings in a memo to your employer.

Telephone special services

There are a number of special telephone services available to subscribers which can benefit a company.

FACT FINDER

Special services to help an organisation

Linkline numbers – these are useful for a company wishing to encourage members of the public to phone them. The 0800 numbers link the caller directly to the Linkline customer who pays for the call. The 0345 numbers allows a caller to contact a Linkline customer from anywhere in the UK for the price of a local telephone call. The Linkline customer pays the balance of the call charge.

Conference calls – up to 60 users can be connected simultaneously throughout the UK and overseas. The user does not require special equipment and this service means that business people do not need to make long, tiring and expensive journeys.

Datel – this service allows computers to communicate with each other over a telephone line.

On-line interpreting – it is possible to obtain the services of an interpreter who is on-line at the same time as you are having a telephone conversation with someone who speaks a different language.

Activity 1.2.5

Your director has heard that cashless calls using a telephone chargecard would improve the telephone facilities for the company's sales representatives when travelling in the UK and abroad. S/he has asked you to find out more about the service and send details to her/him in a memo, as soon as possible.

FACT FINDER

Telephone handset facilities

Most modern telephone handsets have a variety of extra facilities. These may include:

Short code dialling – long telephone numbers may be stored in memory and called up by a specific two- or three- digit code.

Last number recall – by pressing the recall button on the handset a previously engaged number will be dialled automatically.

Call diversion – all calls coming through to one extension may be diverted to another extension until the command is deleted.

Telephone messages

When calls come through for members of staff who are absent there are various alternatives open to the recipient of the call. Either:

1 Obtain the name and number of the caller and arrange for the absent member of staff to call them back; or

2 Ask the caller to phone again at a time when you know the member of staff will be available; or

3 Take a message. Ensure that all the information has been received and that it is correct. Obtain the caller's name, telephone number and message and repeat these to the caller to confirm details. Always pass on messages as soon as possible.

Standard telephone message pads are readily available.

Activity 1.2.6

Use the schedules set out below to record all the telephone calls you make and receive over the next few weeks both at work and home, and if appropriate at your study centre. Give details of the person called or of the call received. Make a note of the reason for the calls and/or any action taken in relation to these calls.

Assess your own competence in making and receiving calls taking into account the telephone techniques already discussed. Also assess the standard of the caller's telephone technique in each case.

Schedule of telephone calls made

Date	Time	Telephone no.	Name of contact	Reason for call	Assessment

Schedule of telephone calls received

Date	Time	Name of caller	Reason for call	Action taken	Assessment

Telephone answering machines

Telephone answering machines are a very useful aid in providing a 24-hour coverage of the telephone system or just to cover lunch hours and short absences from the office.

Some machines have a remote control facility which enables the owner to dial into the machine and 'pick up' any messages which have been left. Some machines are 'answer only' but these are only suitable if you simply wish to give out standard information. Other machines will call you on a pager each time a message is recorded.

Activity 1.2.7

Your director is contemplating installing a telephone answering machine in order that messages may be left in the evenings and over the week-end. S/he is not sure how the system operates or what would happen once a tape has been filled up with messages. S/he has asked you to investigate and put your findings in a memo to her/him.

The investment in new telephone exchanges based on digital technology and the recent use of satellites have resulted in a wider range of telephone communication facilities and services being made available to the business user. In addition, customers now have a more reliable telephone service with better and clearer call connections.

15

Some of these facilities and services are listed below.

Mobile telephones

The advent of the mobile phone has meant that an individual can remain constantly in touch and accessible to others. The executive may take the mobile phone with her/him when travelling between locations, thus ensuring that clients are always in contact, if necessary. Such phones are becoming relatively commonplace on rail, road, sea and air transport. In means that any problems arising in the office can be dealt with immediately.

Voice messaging service

This service allows for a message to be stored in a voice mail box. The 24-hour service enables staff to send, receive or forward messages at any time of the day or night from any telephone world-wide. The messages can be accessed by means of a key pad and personal code.

Modern telephone switchboards

Electronic switchboards provide a wide range of features. In addition to those mentioned under telephone handsets they may have some of the following:

1 Direct dialling inwards – the caller may dial direct to an extension, by-passing the operator.

2 Priority facilities for certain extensions either permanently or for several months.

3 Protected calls for data transmission.

4 Call logging and costs analysis – a computer printout is provided of all or selected calls made from extensions plus their costs.

5 Some extensions 'blocked' – where certain extensions can only be used to dial out to local numbers or cannot be used to receive calls directly from outside the company.

6 Direct access to dictation, paging, public address systems and fire alarms.

7 An intrusion facility allowing someone to 'cut in' on an existing conversation.

8 Self-diagnosis of faults in the exchange and some self-correcting ability.

Activity 1.2.8

You are working in a local manufacturing company which has customers throughout the world. The company has an up-to-date switchboard with 48 extensions installed within the business. All extensions have full dialling facilities.

Your director is appalled at the latest telephone bill which has just arrived. It has increased by 10 per cent on the last bill without any corresponding increase in tariff fees. S/he has asked you to look into the situation and to suggest ways to curb this escalation in costs. Set out your answer in the form of a memo.

As a telephone user it is useful to have as many reference books and as much general information as possible easily available to you. Standard telephone directories together with Yellow Pages are well known to most users but there are other sources of reference which can be invaluable to a frequent telephone user.

Activity 1.2.9

Complete the schedule below showing the various reference books and sources of information useful to a telephone user.

Sources of reference

Source	Contains information on
1	
2	
3	
4	
5	

Element 1.3 – Transmit and receive information using electronic equipment

The investment in digital technology over the past decade and the increased use of communication satellites now allow all types of information – pictures, text, computer data as well as voice – to be transmitted at great speed world-wide.

Some of these communication facilities and services are set out on the following pages.

FACT FINDER

Facsimile transmission

Facsimile transmission, commonly known as fax, is the exact reproduction and transmission to another location of text or drawings over a telephone link. Most machines are capable of both sending and receiving fax documents.

The basic procedure for sending a fax:

1 Find the fax number to be called. There are both national and international fax directories available free to subscribers. The format of fax numbers is the same as for telephone numbers:

International code – country code – area code – local number.

2 Prepare the front page of the fax. This may contain the company logo, in addition to sender and receiver details, and the number of pages in the transmission. This latter item is very important so that the receiver is certain that all pages of the message have been received.

3 The document is placed face down in the fax machine. Check it is correctly positioned.

4 The appropriate fax number is dialled.

5 You will hear a ringing tone. Once connected, the machine, either automatically or after a command by the sender, will transmit a copy of the document to the called machine.

Thus the original document is kept with the sender, a great advantage especially with legal documents. It should be noted that faxes cannot be used as evidence in a court of law.

Most machines will receive automatically so always make sure that there is sufficient paper in your fax machine.

Modern fax machines have many and varied facilities which include:

- Abbreviated dialling – commonly used, multi-digit numbers which can be called with just pressing one or two numbers.

- Automatic redial – the machine will redial automatically if the called machine is engaged.

- Delayed send – the machine can be set to transmit documents left in its document feeder at a specified time to a specified number.

- Polling – the receiving machine initiates the transmission of a document. The sender must know in advance of the transmission and the document must be left in the remote sending machine's document feeder.

- Password polling – similar to above but polling of documents are restricted to those receiving machines with security identification.

- Half-tone transmission – this facility provides different levels of tone thus enabling a clear transmission of photographs and illustrations.

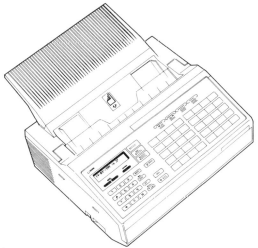

A facsimile machine

Intelpost is the Post Office's high-speed facsimile transmission service and is available at certain Post Offices. If the called person has no fax machine the fax copy may be collected from the Post Office, delivered by special courier service or the copies may be delivered in the post the following day.

Bureaufax is the fax service operated by British Telecom. There are centres throughout the UK where customers may take their faxes or if this is not possible the document may be dictated over the telephone. British Telecom can also arrange for a fax to be sent to a ship at sea via their Inmarsat service.

Both Intelpost and Bureaufax operate nationally and internationally.

Fax transmissions are charged under the same scheme as telephone calls.

International time zones

One factor affecting good communication between and within companies round the world is the time difference. Whilst modern technology has removed some of the problems associated with communication between different time zones it is still useful to know the exact situation should you be calling someone in say New

York on the telephone. It can also prevent a great deal of frustration if you realise there is no reply because the company has closed down for the night.

Activity 1.3.1

Referring to the chart below, you will note that when it is 12 noon in London (Greenwich Mean Time – GMT) it is:

7.00 am in New York   5.00 pm in Calcutta
(- 5 hours GMT)   (+ 5 hours GMT)

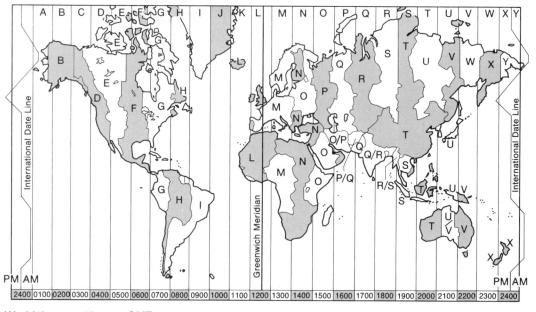

World times at 12 noon GMT

Find out what time it would be in:

- San Francisco, USA
- Rio de Janeiro, Brazil
- Reykjavik, Iceland
- Cape Town, South Africa
- Moscow, Russia
- Tokyo, Japan
- Sydney, Australia.

Set out your answers in tabulated form.

Telex

Telex is used world-wide; there are over one and a half million customers in over 200 countries. In the UK alone there are some 100 000 users. Whilst telex lacks flexibility it is very reliable and although the equipment is quite expensive to buy it may be leased and the actual cost of transmission is relatively cheap.

Modern telex machines can transmit or receive messages completely auto-matically whilst the operator is preparing another message on the display. Incoming messages are stored in memory until the printer is free or priority can be given to an incoming message by pressing the appropriate key.

FACT FINDER

Basic procedure for sending a telex message

1 Find the telex number to be called. There are both national and international telex directories available free to subscribers. For international messages country codes are required.

2 Press the 'Dial/Call' button and check you have a line.

3 Type the required telex number followed by a plus sign. When your call is connected you will receive the answerback code of the called machine. Check that it is correct.

4 Press the 'Here is' key to send your own answerback code.

5 Send your message, which should have been pre-prepared to save time and call charges.

6 When the message is complete, press the 'Here is' key followed by the 'Who are you' key. This confirms that you have been connected to the called machine throughout transmission.

7 Finally 'Clear' the call.

A recent development is teletex or super-telex. This allows users access to the national and international telex networks without the need for a telex terminal of their own. All the teletex user needs is a computer or dumb computer terminal, a modem and a spare telephone line.

Each user is given a unique number with which to send and receive messages. When the user wants to send or retrieve a telex, all s/he needs to do is connect into the teletex switchboard in London via the modem and telephone line. The user can then collect or send messages just as if it were an ordinary office telex terminal.

As well as saving the user the initial cost of a telex terminal, the messages do not have to be sent out in a special form and are sent and received automatically. There is the additional advantage of being able to send and receive teletex messages from the office, home, a hotel or anywhere else where there is access to a computer, modem and telephone line.

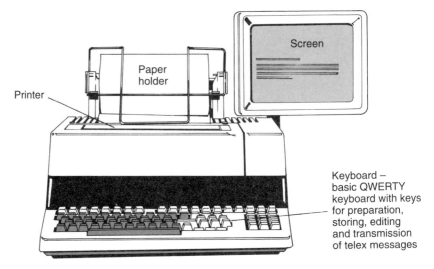

A telex machine

FACT FINDER

Facilities available on modern telex equipment include:

- **Itemised billing** This facility gives details of calls and their separate cost (a useful aid when checking on budgets and over-spending).

- **Multiple broadcasting** This facility will transmit a single message simultaneously to up to ten other telex subscribers. It ensures that the call is made to all parties at the same time. This could be useful when information is being given out about a press release concerning a change in company management or a company takeover.

- **Auto-forwarding call facility** This eliminates unsuccessful calls resulting from engaged lines. The system allows messages to engaged lines to be stored and transmitted once the line is free. A report is sent to the subscriber providing information on call status.

It is possible to send an international telegram and telemessage via a telex terminal as well as sending a telex to ships at sea. British Telecom also offer a service which enables you to have your telex or fax message translated into a foreign language before being transmitted.

Whilst British Telecom have, in the past, provided the main telex service in the UK, Mercury Communications have a telex service which is compatible with UK and international standards and gives a terminal-to-terminal service.

Fax versus telex

There are benefits to be gained and problems which may occur whichever of the main communication systems a company chooses. Many organisations nowadays will buy a fax machine in preference to telex.

The fax machine is more versatile and easier to operate. It is able to send illustrations, for example, drawings and photographs, in addition to straightforward text. There is no need to type out the document, the original is used to produce the digital signals that are transmitted to the receiving machine for conversion into a copy of the original. A compact fax machine with many extra facilities may now be bought quite cheaply. This is of great advantage to the small professional office.

Whilst the number of organisations using fax over the past few years has increased dramatically, telex is still considered by some organisations to be more appropriate for their use and the use of teletex equipment has expanded the scope of the service.

Equipment faults

As a telex or fax operator the need to be able to check for faults and to ensure that the service operates smoothly, is of the utmost importance.

Sometimes with electronic equipment the best action to carry out if a system error appears is to switch off and start again. Often this will clear the fault. Some electronic equipment will have a self-diagnostic program which will locate the type of fault.

If you are involved in operating electronic equipment there are simple guidelines you should follow.

**FACT
FINDER**

Guidelines for the care of electronic equipment

1 Have a copy of the manufacturer's manual kept with the equipment.

2 Clean the equipment regularly.

3 Do not smoke, drink or eat near the equipment.

4 Keep a record of faults and problems and how they were solved.

5 Keep a record of maintenance calls along with status reports.

6 Have your engineer's telephone number at hand. But always check for simple causes of breakdown, for example, a blown fuse, before you call out an engineer.

7 Minimise the movement of equipment. If it is necessary to relocate pieces of equipment then disconnect them from the electricity supply and ensure moveable parts are secure.

Most equipment manuals will give guidance on fault finding. Some examples for a fax machine could be:

Symptom	*Points to check*
The original document does not feed	a) Is the original document torn or curled? b) Is the original document too thick?
The power is ON but the machine does not send	a) Has the document been inserted correctly? b) Does the display show 'DOCUMENT SET'?

Activity 1.3.2

Using the above examples as a guide, prepare a fault solving factsheet for the electronic equipment you are using at your place of work and/or study.

Set out clearly the problems faced by you and your colleagues when operating the various items of equipment and compile a record of equipment faults and how they were solved.

Telemessage

Telemessage is British Telecom's electronic hard copy messaging service. Messages may be sent at any hour from a telephone or telex machine. The messages are delivered in the ordinary post.

Electronic paging

Staff are constantly on the move. They attend meetings at base or away, or maybe visit other members of staff in their offices. Whatever the reason it becomes very difficult for telephone operators and receptionists to contact them. Mobile phones have certainly meant that staff are more accessible, however they are not always convenient, are still comparatively expensive and most are bulky to carry around all day.

One useful device to aid contact is a pager. These are small, lightweight and easily fit into a jacket pocket or bag. Each pager has a unique number which allows the holder to be contacted when away from base. When the holder is required then the pager bleeps. Some pagers have a thin window display which will display a message or the telephone number that the holder should call.

Electronic mail

All of the above systems mentioned in this section could be classed as a form of electronic mail.

Electronic mail is a facility which allows a communication (which may be text or graphics) to be passed electronically between two devices. The devices or terminals create and send the message via a central computer to the receiver's mail box, the central computer storing and processing the message.

If your company subscribes to an electronic mail box service you will be allotted a personal electronic mail box password or number. You should access the mail box on a regular basis as in addition to sending messages to other subscribers to the system you will also receive messages which you will need to deal with. These messages may be scanned or read from any terminal provided the correct password or number is known.

The use of electronic mail systems is becoming more widespread and paper-based memoranda are being replaced by electronic messages left at work stations.

Subscribers to services such as BT's Telecom Gold or Mercury Communications' Link 7500 have instant access to both telex and fax users via their mailboxes.

Activity 1.3.3

You work at a company where your employer is interested in installing an electronic mail system. Investigate such a system and in a memo to your employer set out details of the system including information on how it operates, any special equipment, 'extra' facilities provided and its cost.

Work-related tasks

UNIT

1

You are working for a business involved in the manufacture of reproduction antique furniture which is sold both in the home market and abroad. In fact, as a company you have been extremely successful in cornering the American market.

You work as an administrative assistant to the sales director, Peter Wolfson.

TASK ONE – Elements 1.1, 1.2 and 1.3

You receive the following memo from your employer:

```
M E M O R A N D U M

TO: You (Administrative Assistant to Peter Wolfson)

FROM: Peter Wolfson, Sales Director

DATE: 12 November 199-

COMMUNICATION
```

I am becoming extremely concerned at our slow response to our customers' requests. At a recent conference in Baltimore, some of our overseas clients complained about the difficulties they faced when trying to contact company staff about problems or orders.

I have decided it is necessary that we look very carefully at the communication facilities we have operating in the company.

Telephone facility

Our telephone switchboard needs modernising. The present one has too few lines and we have not been able to expand it to meet all our needs.

It would also be useful to fit a new telephone answering machine. Our present model is quite old and has none of the features of the new machines.

We can afford to spend to ensure that we provide a fast, efficient service to both old and new customers.

Postal facility

Our postal facility also requires attention. Letters are going astray, customers are receiving letters with the wrong enclosures and the wrong services are being used.

I believe we should now contemplate having a central mail room with specialist staff who would ensure that all mail was correctly processed.

We must also install a fax machine as a matter of some urgency. I used to have one in the last company where I worked and it was most useful. We need to fax quotes to customers world-wide and for them to be able to fax back their orders to us.

Please let me have a short report on these matters together with any new procedures you think we should implement. Please include an estimate or the costs involved, within a budget of £15000. You might like to think of delegating some of the research to your junior.

Peter Wolfson

TASK TWO – Element 1.2

If you are not able to develop completely practical competence in the work place you may wish to set up some role-playing situations.

Role-playing situation suggestions

You will need at least two other people to help you with these situations plus a switchboard and two extensions.

Remember to keep a telephone log of the calls you make and receive.

You are working as an administrative assistant for a firm of accountants which has many branches throughout the country. You are on the rota for reception/enquiries which also involves telephone duties.

Whilst you should make some of the calls yourself, you should delegate at least two of the calls to be made by another person and monitor that caller's performance.

Make up any other information you think you require.

1 Phone Ms Singh of the training division informing her that you will be attending the accounting course on Wednesday 14 February 199-. Check that the course starts at 2.00 pm.

2 You are arranging a meeting for Tuesday 20 February 199- at 10.00 am and you need to book the board room and also to arrange the refreshments.
    a) You book the room through the managing director's secretary, Miss Peters.
    b) You book the refreshments with Mrs King in the restaurant.

3 Make a telephone call to Trafford & Trafford stating that goods which were ordered over four months ago have still not arrived. The company was promised a three months' delivery date and the situation is now quite critical.

4 You contact The Travel Shop to arrange a flight for your manager, Mrs H Jenson, to New York on Monday 14 October 199-. She needs to arrive in New York by lunch time (local time).

5 You contact the secretary to the Business Association and apologise that your executive, Mr Wolfson, will not be attending the meeting on Friday 12 June 199- at 2.00 pm.

6 You phone the bank complaining about not having received a bank statement for two weeks. The company normally receives one every week.

Researching and retrieving information

Main elements covered

2.1 Use and develop manual and computerised filing systems
2.2 Locate and abstract information from unspecified sources
2.3 Organise and present information in a variety of formats

Supplementary elements covered

5.1 Produce text from oral and written material using an alphanumeric keyboard
5.2 Present narrative, graphic and tabular information using an alphanumeric keyboard

Element 2.1 – Use and develop manual and computerised filing systems

The test of an efficient filing system is whether or not documents and information requested can be located easily and quickly by anyone. In the past, most information was in paper form, but today information may be received in an office from a range of sources and in a range of forms, for example, magnetic tape, disks or microfiche. Items need to be stored in a way appropriate to their use.

To set up an effective, working filing system, whether manual or computerised, takes time and planning in the initial stages.

Points to consider when creating or changing a manual filing system include the following:

1 What type of equipment is best – vertical, lateral, horizontal or rotary – see the diagrams on the following pages? Is ancillary equipment such as collators, binders, etc required?

2 What classification should be used – alaphabetic, numeric, subject, geographic or alphanumeric – see the diagrams on the following pages?

3 Will an index be required?

29

4 Will colour coding be used to aid retrieval?

5 Where are files to be sited – centrally, departmentally or elsewhere?

6 Regarding the staffing of the system, who will have access? Who will be in overall control of the system?

7 What security methods will be used?

8 What operational procedures will be used?

FACT FINDER

Manual filing equipment

Vertical filing cabinets Files are stored in drawers with the material placed in folders suspended in pockets from side bars. Title strips are fixed to the top of pockets allowing for easy retrieval.

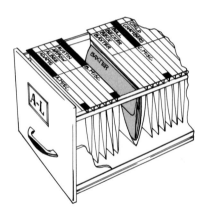

Vertical filing

Horizontal filing cabinets The filing material is placed flat in shallow drawers. This type of system is suitable for maps, drawings and large plans.

Horizontal filing

Lateral filing cabinets Files are stored side-by-side in a cupboard (like books on a library shelf). Sometimes they are held in pockets suspended on overhead rails. Title strips are fixed to the front edge of the files for easy recognition.

Lateral filing

Rotary filing equipment There is a wide range of rotary systems. A basic system may consist of tiers of files fixed to a central spine. Title strips are fixed to the front edge for easy retrieval.

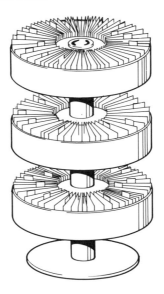

Rotary filing

Filing classifications

The classification used to store material is critical for easy retrieval. It is important that an appropriate one is selected to ensure the system is successful. The main classifications are given below. However some organisations may use a combination of the basic types, for example, alphanumeric where the main classification is alphabetic with numerically-sequenced files within each alphabetic section.

Alphabetic This is a very common way to classify material. The material is filed under the name of the correspondent.

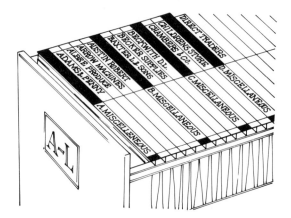

Alphabetic filing

Numeric Either the main reference on a document is numeric, as with an invoice, or an alphabetic title is given a numeric cross-reference. This method has more scope for expansion that a purely alphabetic system.

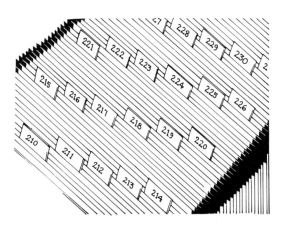

Numeric filing

Subject The material is filed alphabetically but the subject of the document determines its place in the system.

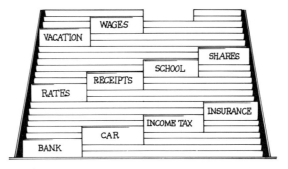

Subject filing

Geographic The material is filed according to the location of the sender of the document. Divisions may be towns, regions, counties or countries depending on the material being stored.

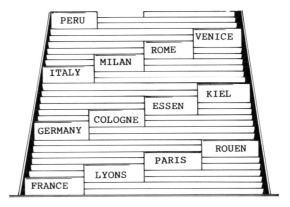

Geographic filing

Chronological With such a system the material is filed in date sequence. Correspondence filed in a file which is classified alphabetically will normally be filed chronologically, with the most recent item appearing on top.

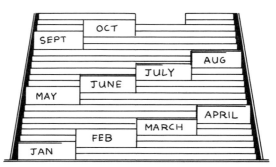

Chronological filing

Activity 2.1.1

Investigate a manual filing system in use and set out a fact sheet on this system under points 1 to 8 mentioned on pages 29–30. Give clear details of the equipment and the operational procedures in use.

From your research would you recommend any improvements to the system being used?

FACT FINDER

The most important features of a good filing system whether manual or computerised are:

1 The system should be *simple*. If the system is too complicated then staff will either not use the system at all or fail to use it correctly.

2 The system must be *suitable* for the organisation. What is appropriate for one organisation could be impracticable for another.

3 The system should be *economical* and be able to be run at the lowest cost compatible with an acceptable degree of efficiency.

4 The system should be capable of *development* and *expansion*. Any minor changes should be accommodated easily.

5 Files should be *secure* from fire, theft or vandalism.

6 *Confidentiality,* where necessary, should be able to be observed. It may be that limited access is given to certain areas of the filing system. In other systems certain information may be held in specialist offices, for example, the personal staff records may be kept in the personnel department under the control of the personnel manager, or the agenda and minutes of board meetings may be held by the managing director's personal assistant.

Activity 2.1.2

Find out the prices of basic manual filing equipment, giving prices from at least three different suppliers. Display this information in a memo to your supervisor, using today's date.

A company's filing may be organised on a departmental basis or be arranged as a central service. There are advantages and disadvantages with whichever system is used. One benefit from organising filing on a central basis is that specialist staff may be employed to run the service, leading to more control and uniformity of filing. However, a central system may cause problems with confidential files.

Activity 2.1.3

Your employer is horrified at the proliferation of filing cabinets that are appearing throughout the offices. S/he has heard that a centralised filing system is the answer. In a report to your employer set out the benefits to be gained from switching from a departmental to a central system but also mention any problems that are likely to occur.

Whichever system is used it is essential to have proper procedures laid down to ensure its efficiency. Whilst the details may vary from company to company the basic rules should always be followed.

Activity 2.1.4

You are supervising the central filing system for a small company. You have several young clerks and students on work experience in to help with running the system. However they have little knowledge of rules and procedures.

Set out, on an information sheet to them, simple rules and procedures to follow when working in the central filing unit.

Some of the material stored by an organisation will be of a confidential nature. The points set out below will give you a guide as to how to ensure that confidentiality is maintained.

FACT FINDER

Confidentiality of information

1 Mark all confidential files and documents clearly giving their level of security.

2 Ensure that confidential files are stored away in locked cabinets when not required and that there is no unauthorised access.

3 Never delegate the copying of confidential documents and never take photocopies superfluous to immediate needs.

4 When working on confidential files work somewhere private and discourage visitors.

5 Never leave confidential documents lying on a desk in clear view of passers-by.

6 Use a shredder for destroying confidential documents. Only burn documents if you (or someone else in authority) is personally able to supervise the operation.

Microfilm systems

Microfilming has been used in offices for many years. It is a process whereby very small photographs of documents are stored on reels of film or on fiche so that they may be used for subsequent reference. The bulky originals can either be destroyed or stored off-site, freeing valuable office storage space.

The main systems are:

1 Microfilm – the image is produced on strips of film which is stored on reels or cassettes. This system is appropriate for inactive files as retrieval of images is slow.

2 Jacket systems – here the separate microimages are placed in transparent pockets. One standard microjacket sheet, measuring approximately 4 inches by 6 inches, would hold 60 × A4 sheets in microfilm form. This leads to much easier retrieval.

3 Aperture card systems – mainly used for storing plans or technical drawings. Each image is framed in a punched card. The code punched into the card will aid retrieval from storage.

4 Fiche systems – these are sheets of film, the standard size measuring 105 mm × 148 mm. The number of images contained on each fiche will vary depending on the degree of microphotography.

Microfilm equipment

Whilst some firms may purchase their own microfilmer or camera equipment other firms will rely on a bureau to film and process their documents. The camera used will depend on the type of system required.

Regardless of whether a company chooses a bureau to film and process its documents it will require some kind of retrieval facility. This is in the form of a microfilm reader and the type chosen will depend on whether the system is film, microjacket, aperture card or fiche. Many microfilm readers will also have a print facility to obtain a hard copy of the image.

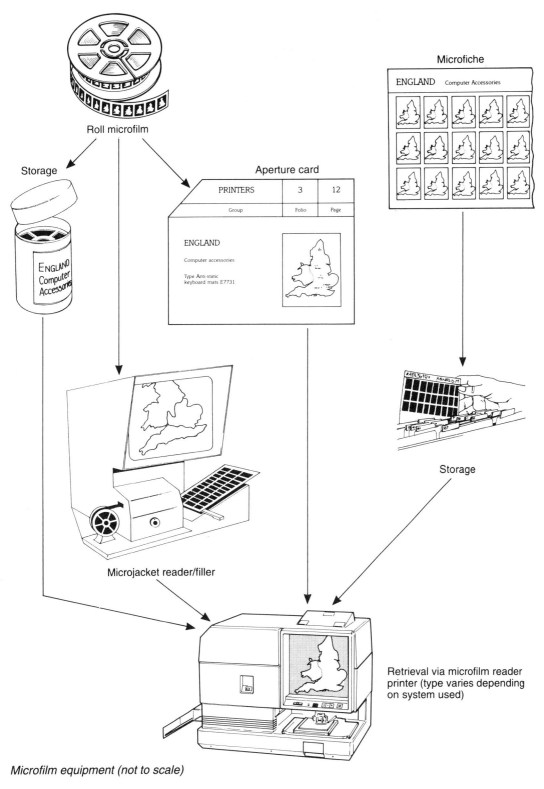

Microfilm equipment (not to scale)

Activity 2.1.5

Find out the main advantages to be gained when an organisation decides to use a microfilm system. Are there any problems from using microfilm?

Conduct a survey of at least six local firms to determine whether or not they use a microfilm system. Set out your answer on a fact sheet.

Whilst film, jacket and aperture card systems are used by many firms the microfiche system is widely adopted by organisations with a high volume of information to be stored.

It is possible for computer output to be directly transferred to microfilm by a process known as COM (Computer Output on Microfilm). Such an operation gives a much faster and more easily handled output than with hard copy.

Computers may also be used in the storage and retrieval of microfilmed documents. Computer Assisted Retrieval (CAR) equipment has a built-in microprocessor which is capable of locating where it is stored when a microfilm reference is keyed in.

Computerised filing systems

There are two main types of computerised filing systems:

1 The user keys in the requested file's number. The system then locates the shelf containing the file and moves that shelf to the front of the machine. A light bar will then illuminate, indicating the position of the file for removal. Traditional paper-based files are still used. The microprocessor is used to locate the file or document.

2 By using scanning equipment documents are quickly and easily converted into images which are stored on disks. Some systems use optical disks for storage which are capable of holding well over 10 000 A4 pages. Disks may be erasable or non-erasable.

When a document is required the appropriate index number is keyed in via a computer program. The requested document image is then displayed on screen and a hard copy obtained, if required, either at the user's work station or it may be transmitted and printed out at a remote location.

Scanners are now available which digitise documents stored on microfilm thus saving on storage capacity. It is claimed that the use of microfilm alongside document image processing prevents bottlenecks as microfilmed images can be scanned much faster than the original hard copy.

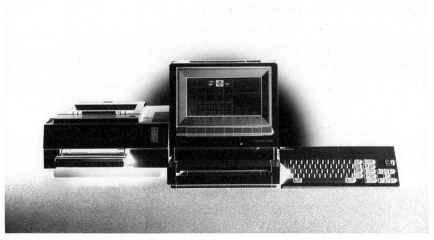

Canofile 250 computerised filing system

Activity 2.1.6

Contact an appropriate supplier or attend a trade computer exhibition to determine the various features offered with a specific electronic filing system. Set out your findings in a memo to your supervisor.

As with a manual filing system an appropriate classification for files and documents is required. Good house-keeping practice is essential to ensure 'dead' files do not clog the system or cause problems with retrieval.

Rules may vary depending on the system used, but some may be:

1 Have a hard copy of all disk directories of files and update these regularly.

2 Have an agreed policy for file retention and review this as necessary (see below).

3 Delete files only in accordance with this policy. (This is assuming that erasable disks are in use and files are capable of being deleted.)

Activity 2.1.7

Using the above rules as a starting point, prepare a full set of rules for members of staff using a computerised filing system to ensure that all files and documents are retrieved easily and quickly, and are not lost or damaged in the system.

Set out your set of rules on an information sheet to be placed on the office notice board.

Database software

Another aspect of computerised filing is the use of database software to store large quantitites of items of information similar to that which might be found on a traditional card index.

This type of software is particularly well suited to storing information such as:

- personal staff records
- customers' details
- suppliers' details
- stock records.

Once the file of information has been created it may be interrogated to reveal and isolate specific details. For example, once all your staff personal details have been entered and stored on file an interrogation may locate in seconds:

1 How many earn over £20 000?

2 How many live in a particular town?

3 How many are over a certain age and coming up for retirement?

4 The names of staff working in a particular department.

Activity 2.1.8

Find out if any database software is used at either your place of work or study. Find out what the software is called and for what type of records it is used.

Retention rates

Legislation may determine how long companies retain certain documents. Where there are no legal requirements companies will determine their own policy. It is important that papers which are not required do not clog up the system. It is equally important that documents which *may* be required in the future are not destroyed.

FACT FINDER

Examples of typical guidelines for retention rates for documents

Internal memoranda	12 months
General correspondence with customers and suppliers	Two years
Banking documents – general	Six years

Sales invoices and credit notes	Six years
Staff records – general	Six years
Company statutory records	Permanently
Property records, title deeds	Permanently

Whilst a court will normally request the original document in evidence, if this cannot be produced then an authenticated microfilm copy of the document is likely to be accepted.

Activity 2.1.9

Find out if there is a document retention policy in operation in the company where you work. Find out the different retention times for the various documents and set out this information in tabular form on a fact sheet.

Data Protection Act 1984

Any organisation involved in processing personal details on a computer is required to be registered with the Data Protection Registrar. Individuals have the right to access and check any data held about them on computer and to have it removed or amended as necessary. There are exemptions to this 'right of access', such as to the police database used for law enforcement.

(See also Unit 5.)

Activity 2.1.10

Investigate the Data Protection Act and set out on a fact sheet all its main provisions under appropriate headings. Include in your fact sheet how an individual would find out who keeps personal data on computers and how s/he could complain if they did not like the way a data user was operating.

Element 2.2 – Locate and abstract information from unspecified sources

You may frequently be required to find out specific information for a member of staff. To ensure success you need to determine:

What information is being requested. Always ensure that you know exactly what is being requested, otherwise you may spend many wasted hours searching for unnecessary facts.

Where you can find this information. There is a wide range of reference books available for the office. It may be that you need to put in a request for specific reference books if these are not available in your office but are required on a regular basis. Otherwise your local library should have a comprehensive stock of such books.

FACT FINDER

Some useful basic reference books to have in the office are:

1 A local *A–Z* gives detailed street maps of the whole area.

2 A *British Rail Timetable Guide* gives timetables of all inter-city and local trains; revised annually.

3 The *ABC Worldwide Hotel Guide* provides information on hotel accommodation throughout the world; revised six-monthly.

4 *Croner's Office Companion* provides a range of up-to-date information including travel, office management, health and safety, entertainment and employment (legislation, financial information, politics and communications).

5 A good atlas including a gazeteer.

6 A good dictionary.

7 *Roget's Thesaurus* which is useful to help you find a word or phrase when composing your own letters and reports.

8 Local telephone directories together with *Yellow Pages* and the *Thompson Directory* (if available in your region).

Activity 2.2.1

Apart from reference books there are numerous other sources of information. Local and national government offices can be a useful source and databases, accessed via Prestel or private viewdata services, are available for general or specialist use.

List as many other information sources that you can think of (including local phone numbers where possible) and set these out on a fact sheet, stating the specific type of information each source provides.

Element 2.3 – Organise and present information in a variety of formats

The way information is presented has a marked effect on the recipient. There are a number of aids on the market to enhance the presentation of information. These include magnetic boards and calendars, plastic boards to use with different coloured markers or electronic notice boards.

Listed figures in particular may be hard to understand or even meaningless, but when presented in graph form the information is more readily interpreted.

Graphs

Graphs may now be created easily and professionally on a computer through a spreadsheet program. Whether the graph is prepared manually or electronically it is necessary for the graph to have a meaningful title and for all items to be clearly labelled.

FACT FINDER

Line graphs may be used to show almost any kind of statistical data, for example, sales or profit figures. The graph may be either single or multi-line depending on the information that needs to be displayed.

Ensure that both the horizontal and vertical axes are clearly labelled and give a key so that there is no misunderstanding the data and what it represents.

When creating a graph remember that the horizontal axis takes the factor which does *not* change whilst the factor which does change takes the vertical axis.

Home and overseas sales for the months of January–June 1992 in £s

	Jan	Feb	Mar	April	May	June	Total
Home	150 000	200 000	250 000	290 000	150 000	150 000	1 190 000
Overseas	230 000	250 000	300 000	400 000	350 000	250 000	1 780 000
TOTAL	380 000	450 000	550 000	690 000	500 000	400 000	2 970 000

These figures have been used to prepare the line graph on page 44.

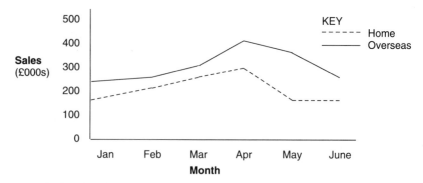

Line graph showing the home and overseas sales figures for January–June 1992

Bar graphs are also an effective way of displaying statistics, but individual 'bars' or 'blocks' are used rather than a continuous line.

The same figures used to prepare the line graph above may just as easily be shown on a bar graph.

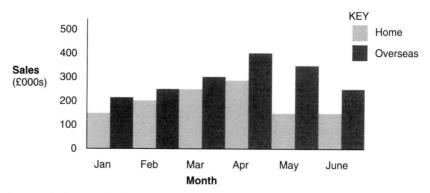

Bar graph showing the home and overseas sales figures for January–June 1992

Pie charts

Pie charts are formed by using a circle, which represents the whole amount, and splitting it up proportionally to represent the separate amounts. An example would be a pie chart showing the total budget for a project and showing proportionally the different amounts that make up the whole budget. The example given shows a comparison between the home and overseas sales as displayed in both the line and bar charts above.

Pie chart showing total home sales and overseas sales for January–June 1992

Charts and graphs

The main use of charts and graphs is:

1 To enable complicated facts and figures to be conveyed quickly and simply.

2 To make it easier to compare 'like with like', for example, sales for one year can be plotted against sales figure for the following year. A graph will show a trend over a period of time.

3 To act as an urgent visual reminder.

4 To give a variety of presentation methods so adding interest to the information.

The use of computer software, in particular spreadsheets, to prepare graphs accurately has greatly enhanced the presentation of work done in the office.

Activity 2.3.1

You have been asked to construct a bar chart for a meeting this afternoon. The chart is to show a comparison of the last three years' sales figures for the six sales regions of Rainers Distributors PLC. Use a graphics package on a computer if possible.

	1988	*1989*	*1990*
	£	£	£
North East Region	871 000	876 000	868 000
North West Region	770 000	772 000	760 000
Central North Region	965 000	960000	952 000
Central South Region	773 000	650 000	610 000
South East Region	654 000	589 000	577 000
South West Region	865 000	765 000	655 000

Tabular format

A common way to display figures is in tabular form (see Activity 2.3.1 above).

For a typist it is quite a difficult operation to ensure that complicated tabular work is set out correctly. The computer operator has the advantage of using the software package to calculate the most appropriate layout.

Activity 2.3.2

Using the tabular format in Activity 2.3.1, type up the column and figures using a spreadsheet or word-processing program.

In addition:

1 Add a column to the right showing the totals for the regions over the three years.

2 Add a total line showing the total for all regions for each year.

A whole range of graphics can now be created quite easily with the use of a Desk Top Publishing (DTP) package.

Activity 2.3.3

Investigate a DTP package, for example, *First Publisher* or *Fleet Street Editor* and create or obtain printouts of some of the graphic and pictorial figures such packages are capable of producing.

Using DTP software, prepare a front cover suitable for your Administration Level 3 file. Use different styles and pitch for the title and other items of information, and enclose the text in a border.

Reports

Reports, both formal and informal, are a common method of conveying information. In a business, a report is usually prepared after an investigation into a situation has been completed.

A **formal report** has the following components:

1 Title page or heading.

2 Terms of reference – this section includes the purpose of the report and why, when and who gave the instructions for the report to be prepared.

3 Procedure – this section gives the procedure followed by the individual(s) carrying out the investigation, for example, interviews, observation, questionnaire.

4 Findings – this section sets out in detail what was discovered during the investigation. Headings should be used as appropriate.

5 Conclusion – this section gives a summary of the findings and the conclusions reached by the author(s).

6 Recommendations – this section gives possible ways of solving the problems encountered in the investigation.

7 Appendices (if appropriate).

A **memorandum report** used for less formal internal reporting generally has three main sections with headings and sub-headings used as appropriate:

1 A description of the background to the problem/situation outlined.

2 An explanation of how the problem/situation was investigated and analysed.

3 A statement of the options available to resolve the problem/situation.

Example of a short, formal report

CONFIDENTIAL

For the attention of the Managing Director – Mr S A Friend

REPORT ON GATEHOUSE SECURITY PROCEDURES AT LONGMORE TECHNICS

1   TERMS OF REFERENCE

In response to complaints from clients and concern from members of management the Managing Director requested the Health and Safety Committee to investigate the situation and to report back by Friday 12 February 199-.

2   PROCEDURE

In order that a clear and accurate picture of the situation could be obtained the following investigatory procedures were followed:

a)   A random selection of staff were interviewed over a period of one week.

b)   A random selection of visitors were interviewed over the same week.

c)   Questionnaires were sent out to all staff requesting their comments on security matters.

d)   The gatehouse staff were interviewed.

e)   Gatehouse procedures were observed on five separate occasions for a total of five hours during one week.

3   FINDINGS

General staff - It appears that staff do not 'sign in'. If the gatehouse staff are otherwise occupied then staff sometimes just slip through without anyone acknowledging their arrival.

Visitors - There is a 'signing-in' book for visitors and the procedure is that they should be issued with a special pass. However, this does not always happen. Passes are not referenced and if visitors are well-known then no pass is issued. Several passes appear to have been mislaid.

Gatehouse staff - Claim they are understaffed. There are just two of them. If one of them is off sick or on holiday there is no one else to help with 'cover'.

4   CONCLUSIONS

The conclusions drawn from the investigation confirm the suspicions on lax security in the company so far as the gatehouse facility is concerned. Staff are not always being visibly 'checked in' and sometimes visitors are not being issued with passes.

5   RECOMMENDATIONS

In order to improve security at the gatehouse it is recommended that the following measures be considered:

a)   An extra member of staff be employed to work in the gatehouse.

b)   A new 'numbered pass' procedure be implemented for *all* visitors.

c)   All general staff to 'sign in'. Special equipment to be purchased.

Signed

Chair - Health and Safety Committee

Activity 2.3.4

You work as an administrative assistant in the general office of an exporting company which is located on an industrial estate on the edge of town. Due to the overcrowded public transport facilities in the rush hour you have been asked to investigate the use of flexitime in the office as a way of alleviating this problem for staff.

Prepare a short memorandum report on your findings.

<table>
<tr><td>UNIT
2</td></tr>
</table>

Work-related task

You work for a firm of insurance brokers. Business has increased considerably over the past couple of years, so much so that it is becoming increasingly difficult to locate documents.

TASK ONE – Elements 2.1, 2.2 and 2.3

You receive the following memo:

M E M O R A N D U M

TO: You (Administrative Assistant)

FROM: Ronald Rushton

DATE: 18 November 1992

FILING SYSTEMS

You are aware of the problems we face with storing all our documents safely and where they can be easily retrieved. Your comments concerning the use of microfilm or an electronic filing system in the company are very sensible. Despite the costs I think we should look carefully into such a proposition as I am sure in the long term a change would provide a better service to our customers.

Would you please investigate this subject further and supply me with details of systems and costs for both electronic filing and microfilm.

Check to see if we could reduce the number of items that we hold at present. Please obtain details of our legal obligations so far as retention times for documents are concerned.

Set out all your findings in the form of a report so that I can present it to the Management meeting next month. Please include any security and confidentiality procedures we should implement with the new system.

Many thanks

Ron Rushton

Reception

Main elements covered

3.1   Receive, screen and assist visitors

Supplementary elements covered

5.1   Produce text from oral and written material using an alphanumeric
keyboard

5.2   Present narrative, graphic and tabular information using an
alphanumeric keyboard

Element 3.1 – Receive, screen and assist visitors

When someone enters an office usually the first person they see is the receptionist. As the receptionist is the first representative of the company to any visitors it is of the utmost importance that s/he makes a good impression.

Many large companies employ a full-time receptionist whose only duty is to receive, assist and direct callers. In smaller businesses this work is often combined with telephone and general office duties.

Activity 3.1.1

Your company has expanded and it has decided to employ a full-time receptionist.

1 What qualifications and qualities would you expect from applicants and what are the duties involved?

2 Prepare the advertisement to be placed in your local newspaper.

An organisation can expect a range of callers which may include customers, suppliers, visitors and the personal friends and family of employees. It is good practice for a receptionist to learn the names of frequent callers, but be sure to use the correct pronunciation. It is likewise good practice for the name of the receptionist to be clearly shown, either on a badge to be worn or on a name stand displayed on the reception desk.

A receptionist must always be polite and friendly but should be very careful not to divulge any company information to visitors. S/he should be careful not to be drawn into long conversations with callers, it is always safer 'not to know'.

Visiting cards

Most business people will have visiting cards which give details of the caller and their company. The information on the visiting card saves the receptionist asking too many questions of the visitor. A computerised or manual card index of callers' names and important facts about them is a useful aid to good reception work. The information on the visiting card can be used to prepare such a guide.

A manual card index

Activity 3.1.2

Your company employs a full-time receptionist but there are times when a 'stand-in' is required. In order that anybody deputising for the receptionist maintains the good image of the organisation, draft some guidelines to assist newcomers to reception work. In particular, refer to taking messages, both verbally and in writing, and the need always to keep records up-to-date, legible and accurate.

It is important that the receptionist has a full knowledge of the structure of the organisation and the names of the senior executives of the company. A chart showing such details would be useful and enable the receptionist to refer a visitor to a deputy should an executive not be available.

Activity 3.1.3

If you have not already worked through the activities for Unit 1 prepare a simple organisation chart of the establishment where you work or study. Research the names of all the main officers and their deputies, and their main responsibilities.

If you have carried out such a task (under Activity 1.2.1), make a photocopy and place it with your reception notes.

Brochures and leaflets on company products are frequently held in reception. One of the duties of the receptionist is to see that they are attractively displayed and replaced when torn or out-of-date. A receptionist should make her/himself fully aware of the company's business.

It is also very useful for a receptionist to know the basic type of work being carried out in the various sections/departments of the company. This should increase the help and advice s/he can give to visitors to the organisation.

Activity 3.1.4

Personnel, accounts, sales, purchasing, general administration and production are six sections in the organisation for which you work.

Make lists of the type of work you would expect to be carried out in each section. To which section would you refer visitors wanting information on:

1 A query on an invoice.

2 A sales representative.

3 A job vacancy.

4 A quotation for goods.

Some visitors will arrive at reception without an appointment. A receptionist may need to be very tactful to ensure a successful outcome and that the caller does not leave with a bad impression of the organisation.

Activity 3.1.5

A personal friend of the managing director arrives. He wishes to see her/him but has no appointment. The managing director is busy with important clients. What would you do and say?

A very clear record of all visitors should be kept. There are standard visitors' books available on the market. Some companies prefer to have their own style. The information contained in such a register may be most useful if a member of staff wishes to check dates and times of callers, but it is also essential information in the event of a fire or emergency to know who is on the premises.

Reception Register

Date _____

Time	Visitor's name	Company	Appointment with	Visitor's signature	Time of dep.	Pass recd. by

Reception register (where passes are issued)

Activity 3.1.6

There was an emergency in reception and it was necessary for you to be absent. A young recruit 'stood in' for you at a moment's notice. In your absence, the junior jotted down notes of callers. Sort out these notes and record them in a reception book.

What should you say to the junior if such an occurrence happens again?

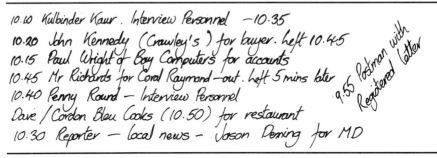

10.10 Kulbinder Kaur. Interview Personnel −10.35
10.20 John Kennedy (Crawley's) for buyer. Left 10.45
10.15 Paul Wright of Bay Computers for accounts
10.45 Mr Richards for Coral Raymond −out. Left 5 mins later
10.40 Penny Round − Interview Personnel
Dave / Cordon Bleu Cooks (10.50) for restaurant
10.30 Reporter − local news − Jason Deming for MD
9.55 Postman with Registered letter

Notes

Reception Register

Date _____

Time	Visitor's name	Company	Appointment with	Visitor's signature	Time of dep.

Security

Many receptionists will be at the forefront of security procedures with visitors. In most organisations there are strict rules preventing unauthorised entry.

Some companies stipulate that identity passes are worn by staff at all times. Visitors are issued with a pass on arrival and checked out on departure. Often visitors do not gain access past reception. Interview rooms are located close to reception and any business is carried out there.

If you are directing a visitor to another department always ensure that s/he is escorted at all times. Do not allow a visitor to wander round the company premises by themselves. Likewise, you should never leave a visitor alone in a room where there are confidential papers or documents. If you have to leave the room slip the papers quietly out of the way before leaving and ask someone else to take your place in the office. Staff should always be aware of the security gap when visitors enter an office and should shield VDU screens and documents from a visitor's view.

Activity 3.1.7

Your employer is concerned about staff being lax about security at one of the company's branches. As your face is unknown at this branch s/he has asked you to check out the situation.

This is what you found:

● When you arrived at the branch office in the morning you walked straight past the reception desk. No one stopped you although as a visitor you should have been requested to sign the visitor's book.

● You then made your way to the main administration offices. There were people in the corridor but again no one stopped you. In the manager's office you could hear the sound of dictation so you walked into a side office. The petty cash box was open on the desk and the filing cabinet was unlocked, the computer was switched on with the screen showing the minutes of yesterday's board meeting.

● Later you walked through the personnel department where you were able to see confidential personnel records lying on a desk.

You reported back to your supervisor and s/he has asked you to draft a memo to branch staff setting out guidelines on security and visitors, and the rules they should follow to ensure that their work is kept safe and confidential.

Occasionally there may be unwanted callers to your company who may be abusive if they do not get their way. Always be firm and polite, never lose your temper. Do not aggravate the situation.

Activity 3.1.8

You are the receptionist at a large local company and a sales representative from a firm selling office furniture calls. S/he is most insistent that s/he wishes to see the buyer who you know is very busy and does not like to see anyone without an appointment. What will you do and say?

Your role

As an administrative assistant, whether or not you are asked to work on the main reception rota, it is still likely that part of your role will be to welcome and deal with visitors.

Always greet visitors pleasantly by name (if possible) and give them your immediate attention. If you happen to be on the telephone when a visitor arrives, acknowledge their presence with a smile and finish your call as soon as possible.

You should keep up-to-date with work being carried out in the company and get to know which visitor is connected with which project. This will help you to deal with visitors intelligently and correctly, but take care not to say anything which would cause embarrassment or upset to your employer.

Known and scheduled visitors

Try to positively recognise visitors and use their names if possible. You may also know the reason for their visit and be able to ensure that they are escorted to the appropriate office.

There will be occasions when your employer is delayed, maybe due to heavy traffic or for other reasons. If this occurs there are a limited number of options open to you. If the caller is not able or keen to wait you may be able to deal with the matter yourself or find another member of staff who is able to do so. If you deal with the matter yourself, make sure you do not commit the company to any kind of action without being absolutely sure that you are acting in accordance with company policy. Give your employer written notes of your action.

If callers decide to wait ensure that they have a comfortable seat and are offered some form of reading matter, as well as coffee or tea. Contact them frequently to assure them that you are doing all you possible can to contact your employer and that as soon as s/he arrives you will inform her/him.

Never show visitors straight into your employer's office as s/he may be engaged on the telephone or dealing with some other matter. Alternatively, s/he may want to check particular details about the visitor to ensure that s/he is fully briefed on all information about the visit.

Unless absolutely necessary, avoid interrupting your employer when s/he has visitors. If you must enter her/his office try not to make a disturbance and have any message written out on a piece of paper. It is advisable to check your employer's thoughts on such matters beforehand.

Unknown and unscheduled visitors

If an unexpected visitor calls, the action you take will depend on whether the person is known to you and if you know whether or not they will be welcomed by your employer. Whoever it is, always be polite and helpful and deal with the problem tactfully. Situations change, it may be that your employer will be pleased to see today's unwanted visitor in a few months' time.

Activity 3.1.9

Over the next few weeks draw up schedules for:

● Visitors you greet whether at work, study or home. Record details of their names and where they are from, and any action that was taken as a result of their visits. Assess your own performance in dealing with these visitors. Do you think you dealt successfully with any problems that occurred?

● Your own visits as a caller. Give details of time, date and place of your calls. Assess the performance of those who greeted you. Were they friendly and helpful or were they rude and made you feel uncomfortable?

From your experience you should begin to be able to build up a useful picture of which special attributes make up a good receptionist.

To help you in your appraisal of your own and other people's reception skills you may wish to answer the following:

1 Was the reception desk tidy with message pad, visitors' book, visitors' passes and pen readily available?

2 Were you greeted with a friendly smile and a 'Good Morning/Afternoon/ Evening, may I help you?'

3 Was the purpose of your visit identified by allowing you time to state your business?

4 Were sensible questions asked to clarify the reason for your visit?

5 Was their knowledge of the company used to help you?

6 Was the receptionist over-familiar with you?

7 Did the receptionist exercise tact when telling you that a particular member of staff was not available?

8 Did the receptionist take clear notes of messages to be handed on?

9 Did the receptionist speak clearly and use a tone of voice to convey interest and concern for your needs?

10 Did the receptionist divulge any company confidential information to you?

Visitors

Some visitors are straightforward and easily dealt with, others are much more difficult. Whilst it is difficult to categorise visitors positively it is sometimes useful to recognise the various characteristics that you may be called upon to deal with. Be constantly aware of the visual impact of your appearance and facial expressions.

The persistent questioner

Some visitors take delight in trying to obtain information about matters that do not concern them. Always be wary of such people and if necessary pretend you 'don't know'.

The aggressive, complaining type

Maybe the caller feels s/he has just reason to be aggressive. However, take a deep breath and do not become agressive in turn. Be positive with your speech and firm and friendly in your approach.

If the caller complains about poor service respond by choosing positive phrases such as, 'I understand what you are saying' and then add, 'How can I help you?'

Always attempt to keep the conversation on a cheerful note. Instead of saying, 'What's the matter?' say, 'Please tell me all about it.'

Overseas visitors and non-native speakers

Sometimes overseas visitors are difficult to understand. Be patient and speak slowly. If you know you are frequently going to meet foreign visitors from certain countries it is useful to obtain appropriate language dictionaries and to locate those members of staff who are fluent in, or know, a foreign language.

Disabled visitors

Some may need special attention and facilities. Be aware that a visitor may not be able to climb a flight of stairs or have easy access in a wheelchair. Do not be patronising but try to be as helpful as possible.

The shy, quiet visitor

Some visitors feel overawed by large company reception desks. Use a tone of voice to convey interest and concern for their needs. Make sure that they are not kept waiting whilst other, more pushy visitors are dealt with promptly.

Remember

- Asking questions not only shows that you are listening but it also helps the person you are talking to listen as well.

- Do not label a caller unimportant because s/he is poorly dressed.

- Always look friendly and cheerful. Do not let your personal life interfere with your work.

- Always be aware of the correct protocol when dealing with staff and their relative positions in the company. It is good practice to introduce the most senior (in terms of position) person first. Make sure when you introduce guests that correct titles are given and no one is left unannounced.

- Do not give preferential treatment to certain callers unless their business is urgent or your employer instructs you otherwise.

- Use positive conversation techniques and give the visitor the opportunity to respond. Do not say 'I don't know what you're talking about', instead ask them to 'Please explain that again.'

Activity 3.1.10

Referring to the above points make a schedule of all the unusual and difficult callers that come to reception and that are dealt with by you or your colleagues. Indicate why their visit was not easy. Think carefully about the speech that was used in dealing with these visitors. Was it positive? Were the questions open ended and did they allow the visitor to relate her/his reason for their visit in a relaxed manner?

If possible, discuss the outcome of the caller's visit with your colleagues and think whether it was successful or not.

Work-related task

UNIT
3

You are head of reception and work for a company whose main business is the manufacture of aeroplane parts. The company carries out work which is highly secret and sensitive to espionage. There is, therefore, a high-security profile throughout the company's premises.

The reception desk in the main entrance hall is manned by a team of receptionists as well as having the presence of a security guard. All staff are checked in and out by reception staff.

As part of the general tightening up of security it has been decided to issue staff identity passes and to issue visitors with numbered passes on arrival. Visitors' passes are to be checked back in by reception when visitors leave the premises. All visitors' passes will have to be accounted for at the end of each day.

TASK ONE – Element 3.1

You receive the following memo:

```
M E M O R A N D U M

TO: You (Reception Supervisor)

FROM: Jeff Larson, Office Manager

DATE: 15 May 199-

SECURITY - VISITORS' PASSES

Further to our talk about visitors' passes I would like
you to investigate the kind of passes which we could
purchase or have prepared for us, and the costs. We need
to have the company's logo on the pass.

I would also like you to draft the procedures and
documentation necessary to run the operation
successfully.

Please let me have this as soon as possible. It is
rather important we get these new security procedures
working immediately.

Thanks.

Jeff Larson
```

TASK TWO – Element 3.1

It is a month later and the new security for visitors procedure was introduced this morning. You are helping at the desk to ensure that everything runs smoothly. Enter this morning's visitors in chronological order using the 24-hour clock in the new reception register which you have designed. The first pass issued this morning was to Mr Day, it was number 0001.

The morning's callers were:

Simon Day from the *Daily News* who came to interview the production manager at 9.25 am and left at 11.10 am; Matthew Brown from Office Machines arrived at 9.30 am to see the office manager and left at 10.45 am; Jane Gardner from Gardner Green & Co arrived at 10.05 to see the company secretary and handed in her pass at 11.15 am; Mrs H Kaur signed in to see the personnel officer and left at 10.30 am; Gregorio Perez, a sales agent with the Madrid Branch, arrived at 12 noon to see the sales manager; Doris Fletcher from Telford Domestics Ltd arrived at 12.45 am to report to the restaurant manager; Sir David Blake of Badger Associates kept his appointment with the chief executive at 11.00 am and left at 12 noon; Mr Raj of Dawley Designers had an appointment with the marketing and promotions manager at 12.30 pm and has just handed in his pass. It is now 1.05 pm.

TASK THREE – Element 3.1

You have received the following memo from the other staff on reception.

M E M O R A N D U M

TO: You (Reception Supervisor)

FROM: Reception Staff

DATE: 23 June 199-

RECEPTION TRAINING

All Reception Staff would like to have some further reception training. Whilst we feel we do a good job we also think that if we knew more about the Company's function and products we could assist callers and visitors more than we do now.

We also would like to have a refresher course on reception and telephone techniques and to have formal discussions on how to deal with 'problems'.

We realise it is impractical for us all be out of the office at the same time but are quite prepared to stay on after work or have the training in our lunch hour. Alternatively, some other members of staff could look after reception during a 'quiet' period whilst we receive training.

Please let us know if arrangements can be made.

Prepare the training programme for your reception staff giving details of subject areas covered and time allowed. Send the programme with a memo to your personnel and training department for their approval.

Arranging travel

Main elements covered

4.1 Arranging travel and accommodation

4.2 Plan and organise business visits

Supplementary elements covered

2.2 Locate and abstract information from unspecified sources

2.3 Organise and present information in a variety of formats

5.1 Produce text from oral and written material using an alphanumeric keyboard

5.2 Present narrative, graphic and tabular information using an alphanumeric keyboard

Element 4.1 – Arrange travel and accommodation

Many business people are required to travel with their work and as an administrative assistant you may be expected to make your employer's travel arrangements.

Attention to detail is of the utmost importance whether the visit is local, national or international. The same basic planning routine is required for all visits.

Basic routine

1 Open a file for all the papers connected with the trip – items to do with travel, itinerary, insurance, correspondence, accommodation, reminders, notes on people to be seen and meetings to be attended.

2 Prepare a check-list of matters to be attended to, especially with space for adding notes; this is invaluable. For convenience, details can be written inside the front cover of the file

Activity 4.1.1

Draw up a list of reference books and other sources of information for arranging travel and accommodation both in this country and abroad.

Set out your work clearly, using either a word-processing package or an electronic typewriter, in order that other members of staff may use it as reference.

Itinerary

When your employer leaves on a business trip you should have prepared an itinerary, showing travel arrangements, hotel reservations and business meetings as well as all necessary addresses and phone numbers.

FACT FINDER

An itinerary should set out clearly:

- day and date;

- time of train/flight – departure;

- time of train/flight – arrival;

- time of checking in (airport);

- reservation details, for example, flight/seat number (plane) or ticket/coach/carriage/seat/sleeper berth (train);

- lunch/dinner arrangements where applicable;

- if being met on arrival – where, how and by whom;

- name, address and telephone number and reservation details of hotel;

- time, place and purpose of engagements, with names of main people involved.

Always state clearly which airport or railway station is being used. In some large cities there is more than one and this could lead to confusion with trains or planes being missed. Your employer may also need to travel between a domestic and international terminal in an airport. This can be time consuming and allowances should be made for such journeys when planning an itinerary.

Make sure you have several copies of the itinerary, including one for your file.

	ITINERARY – THURSDAY 6 DECEMBER 199-
0848	Depart Birmingham (first class, restaurant facilities)
1032	Arrive Euston (car from Head Office)
1130	Goran Hotel – meeting with London Director – Mr Preston
1230	Lunch with Mr Preston and Deputy, Mrs Read
1400	Car to new development – Docklands
1600	Sales Managers' Meeting – Goran Hotel – Sales Targets
1740	Car to Euston
1810	Depart Euston (first class, restaurant facilities)
1953	Arrive Birmingham

Example of an itinerary

Modes of travel

Choice will be influenced by several factors including:

- cost

- speed

- availability of appropriate routes

- distance to be travelled

- 'tiring' or stress factor

- comfort factor.

Rail travel

Realistically it will be mainly national rail routes for which you are booking places. However, there will be occasions when foreign railways may be the most appropriate mode of travel. In such circumstances, it may be better to consult your local travel agent.

The main timetables for British Rail trains are: a) *British Rail Passenger Timetables*, published annually and giving schedules for all UK routes; b) The *ABC Rail Guide*, published monthly but giving only the services to and from London; c) *Intercity Guide to Services*, published twice yearly. Additional information is also provided, such as sleeper, rail/drive and catering services.

Activity 4.1.2

You are working in the administrative support services section and a Mr Phillips comes in and asks for your help. Next Friday morning he is going to be in Manchester and he needs to be in London by 1.30 pm at the latest. He wants to be back in Manchester by the Tuesday afternoon.

Look up the information required using the timetable below and type up the information in the form of a memo to Mr Phillips. Also give details of any buffet or restaurant facilities available on the trains suggested.

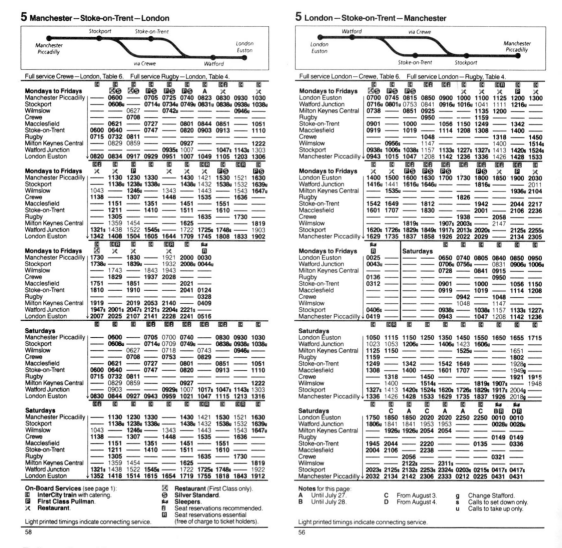

Railway timetable

Air travel

You can book plane tickets either through a travel agent or directly with an airline. Internal flights in the USA may be booked at the US airport just an hour or so before a plane leaves for its destination, if there are spare seats. Whenever you book a plane ticket always make sure you know whether the time given is Greenwich Mean Time (GMT) or local time (see Unit 1 – Activity 1.3.1). Also be aware of international and continental summer time changes.

Activity 4.1.3

When discussing air travel, an airport is frequently referred to by its name rather than the city to which it is attached. We refer to Heathrow rather than London and JFK (John F Kennedy) rather than New York. In fact New York has more than one airport; Newark and La Guardia are also airports close to New York which accept international flights. Washington DC has both the Dulles and National Airports. Similarly with several other cities world-wide.

Prepare a chart of all the capital cities of the European Community and find out the names of their airport(s). Set out your answer in tabulated form under the headings – Country, City, Name of airport(s).

If your traveller has to catch more than one plane it is usually possible to have her/his baggage 'checked in' through to the final destination so that there is no waiting around to collect luggage in the middle of a flight. This could be a great help when there is limited time between flights or when scheduled flights are delayed.

Activity 4.1.4

1 Find the names of at least three car hire firms which operate from Heathrow and Birmingham International Airports. What do they charge per day to hire out a car? Does the price include 'unlimited mileage'? What documentation must the driver provide?

2 Sometimes your employer may wish to drive her/himself to the airport and park the car there. Investigate the car parking fees for both Heathrow and Birmingham International Airports.

It is always advisable to book air tickets well in advance if possible. Remember when preparing international itineraries:

• the effects of jet lag and 'tiring' flights;

• dates of national holidays for the countries to be visited;

• different customs of the country being visited;

• international time differences.

Activity 4.1.5

You are working in the administrative support services of Office Providers Ltd near Heathrow Airport and you are acting as a personal assistant to Marlene Ritchie – a female business executive – who travels extensively all over the world. On arrival this morning you have a note from her asking you to find the times of flights out of Heathrow to New York for tomorrow morning. She would like to leave about mid-morning. What will the local time be on arrival?

(You may use Prestel or similar equipment to find out this information.)

Sea travel

A disadvantage with sea travel is the limit on routes. The *ABC World Shipping Guide* gives details of passenger sailings. However it is unlikely that your employer will choose to travel by sea unless s/he is afraid of flying. Should there be an occasion when a car ferry is to be arranged, book in plenty of time and always check to find out whether a cabin is required.

Car travel

Generally, car travel is not appropriate for long distances, although it is useful if many different locations are to be visited in one day. If international travel is involved always check insurance and local motoring rules. Ensure your employer takes her/his driving licence.

If you need to hire a car for another person find out their preferences, i.e. the make and size of car, the type and whether the driver prefers automatic or manual gears.

Activity 4.1.6

You are based in the centre of London. What modes of travel would you recommend, and what factors would you consider, if you were required to make arrangements for a business trip for your supervisor to the following?

1 Three companies in the centre of London.

2 A town 100 miles away with a stop-over to visit a branch of the company on the way.

3 A company 10 miles from Paris.

4 An international conference in New York.

Set out your answers in the form of a memo to your supervisor.

Accommodation

Finding appropriate accommodation for both your employer and visitors may be an important aspect of your job. With experience, your knowledge of local hotels and their facilities will be invaluable. It is useful to keep a file on such details together with up-to-date prices.

If you need to book international hotels a useful aid is to use hotel chain central agencies who are able to make bookings in hotels belonging to their group throughout the world.

FACT FINDER

Questions to bear in mind when booking accommodation:

1 What are your employer's preferences – 'in' or 'out' of town? Consult your files to see where s/he stayed on previous visits.

2 Is your employer attending a conference at a hotel where s/he would probably want to stay?

3 Is a single or double room required? Must there be en suite facilities?

4 Are there other travellers in the group? Maybe they wish to stay in the same hotel and you will need to liaise with their administration service.

5 Are particular travel facilities required close to accommodation?

6 Do special diets need to be catered for?

7 Is entertainment required?

Activity 4.1.7

You are working in personnel and training and an assistant, Chris Peters, has asked for your help in locating the names and addresses of three hotels in the Birmingham area which have conference and accommodation facilities to hold a maximum of 500 delegates.

Set out your answer in the form of a memo to Chris Peters.

Passports and visas

Ensure your employer's passport is current. A passport is not always sufficient documentation to gain entry to a country. Check whether the country to which s/he is travelling requires a visa and/or entry and exit permits. You may check with the appropriate embassy or a reference book, such as *Croner's Office Companion*, will provide you with the correct details.

A full UK passport is valid for ten years. Should your employer's passport be out of date allow plenty of time to renew it. The main London passport office is at Clive House, 70-78 Petty France. There are also regional passport offices.

Completed application forms should be sent to your regional passport office together with two recent authenticated identical photographs measuring not more than 2½ inches × 2 inches plus supporting documents, for example, birth and marriage certificates. The cost is £15.00 for a basic passport and £30.00 for a 94-page passport (1991 fees).

Other short-term passports are available from the post office but are only valid in certain countries, mainly those belonging to the EC.

Activity 4.1.8

You have just started work at a new firm of financial consultants. Their business involves a certain amount of international travel. One of the junior partners, Pauline Nicholls, is to travel to Iceland in a few days' time but she has no passport.

You have heard there is another type of passport she could use and she has asked you to find out about it, where one could be obtained and how much it would cost.

Another partner will be travelling to Czechoslovakia in a few weeks and she wants to know whether a visa and any other documentation is required for her visit.

Set out the required information on a fact sheet.

Insurance

Comprehensive insurance (including medical, luggage, etc.) should always be obtained for any overseas travel. If travelling by car outside of the UK 'extra' car insurance will be required. There are many good, combined 'travel' insurance packages around but always check the details (particularly the section on exclusions) carefully. Medical bills can be astronomical, especially in the USA.

Short-term travel insurance may be arranged with an insurance broker or through a travel agent. The cost usually depends on the number of days abroad. Some insurance companies will offer business travellers an annual rate of travel insurance.

Types of insurance with typical limits of compensation available

Personal accident – injury or death	£75 000 max.
Medical expenses	£500 000
Cancellation/curtailment of journey	£2 500
Luggage	£2500
Loss of money or travellers' cheques	£750
Personal liability	£500 000 limit
Hijack	£1 400 max.

There are of course conditions and exceptions to these amounts. The small print on an insurance policy should always be read very carefully.

Foreign currency

It is sensible to have a supply of foreign currency when travelling abroad to pay for such items as taxi fares and tips. Always remember to book cash well in advance of the departure date. It is advisable to check whether the country being visited has any restrictions on the amount of money being taken in or out.

Travellers' cheques are a safer way of carrying money while travelling (see also Unit 9). They can be supplied in a wide range of currencies, for example, American dollars, Spanish pesetas, Japanese yen, and may be used as cash if they are made out in the currency of the country being visited.

Activity 4.1.9

You are still working for the financial consultants and your employers have asked you to prepare a fact sheet on travellers' cheques giving details on how they are purchased and how they are used in payment for goods and services.

Set out your findings on an information sheet to all staff arranging travel. In addition, set out other financial services available to business people travelling overseas.

Eurocheques are an easy and safe way to pay for goods and services abroad as are the various credit cards which are now being accepted in an increasing number of countries.

One aspect which should be considered with foreign currency is the rate of exchange being offered when cashing travellers' or Eurocheques, or when using a credit card to obtain cash. This can vary quite considerably between the banks and the numerous bureaux de change.

Banks will sometimes charge a higher commission for cashing cheques and their hours of opening are not as long as most bureaux de change. It is worthwhile checking around to find which agency gives the better rate of exchange. A small percentage difference on a large amount may give a considerable saving overall.

Activity 4.1.10

Find out the rates of exchange for the following countries:

- Australia

- Canada

- Hong Kong

- New Zealand

- South Africa

- USA.

Produce a schedule clearly showing how much of each of these currencies you would obtain for £10, £50, £100, £250, £500, £1000 and £5000.

Medical

If your employer is travelling within the European Community it is advisable to apply for a Certificate E111 from the local Department of Health. This will entitle the carrier to free medical treatment, if required, under the EC reciprocal health service scheme.

Always check whether vaccination certificates are required for the countries being visited. If vaccinations are required arrange for them to be carried out as early as possible as sometimes they can give unpleasant side effects or require booster doses to complete the treatment.

Special medical packs need to be prepared if your employer is travelling to high risk areas, for example, where typhoid or malaria outbreaks are common.

FACT FINDER

The type of items which may be included in a medical kit for a person travelling overseas are:

adhesive dressings; anti-malarial tablets; antiseptic ointment; aspirin; diarrhoea prevention tablets; insect repellant; pain relievers; salt tablets; sunburn lotion; a thermometer; water purification tablets; sterile syringes to reduce the risk of AIDS.

Activity 4.1.11

Mr Gomez, one of the partners in the firm of financial consultants for whom you work, is going to take a business trip to South America. You have been asked to investigate whether vaccinations are required for the following countries:

- Argentina
- Bolivia
- Brazil
- Chile
- Peru and
- Venezuela.

Set out your findings in the form of a memo to Mr Gomez.

Element 4.2 – Plan and organise business visits

If your employer is a frequent traveller you should keep current train and airline timetables in your office. You may use a travel agent but it is useful to have these reference books to check on what is available.

Prior preparation

There may be several tasks you will carry out prior to your employer's journey, whatever the length of the visit, which will ensure that it runs smoothly and all objectives for the visit are met.

1 You may need to write to clients, customers or branch personnel whom your employer may wish to contact. If specific arrangements are made, i.e. time, date and place of meetings, these facts should be given to your employer along with copies of relevant letters, memos, and fax messages relating to appointments and reservations made.

2 Background details of companies to be visited is most important, together with particulars of work transacted with these companies and details of any present work in progress.

3 The papers and documents for any conferences or meetings to be held should be put into a file. Make sure there is nothing missing!

4 An office stationery pack should be prepared, including audio cassettes if required, for use during travel. Ensure that s/he has a sufficient stock of visiting cards.

Other duties

1 **Work to be done in employer's absence**   An employer's visit out of the office is often a good opportunity to 'catch up' on outstanding work. Discuss this with your employer before s/he leaves.

2 **Informing other people/organisations of your employer's absence**   Whether your employer is away for one or ten days, there are always people who need to know. In particular make sure your receptionists/telephonists know of her/his whereabouts and any deputising procedure in operation.

3 **Contact with your employer whilst s/he is away**   If your employer is to be away for any length of time it is advisable to have a 'plan' for contacting her/him at regular intervals.

Activity 4.2.1

Consider the action to be taken when attempting to contact your employer who is:

- at a railway station
- at an airport
- on board a ship
- driving a car.

Set out your answer in the form of a memo to your employer.

Final check-list

It is always useful to make a final check-list of items required for a visit abroad. One with boxes to tick is useful to ensure that no item is left behind which may cause embarrassment or disruption to the journey.

Some of the items on such a check-list may be:

Passport	☐
Visa	☐
Foreign currency	☐
Travellers' cheques	☐
Visiting cards	☐

Activity 4.2.2

Referring to the check-list above prepare a *full* final check-list for an executive travelling on a sales promotions visit to the Middle East.

Taking care of travellers' cheques

1 Keep the record of your cheque numbers and values in a completely different place from the cheques themselves.

2 List the full serial number of each travellers cheque at the time of purchase and tick off when and where they are used. This will be useful if your cheques should be lost or stolen.

3 Never countersign cheques in advance.

Embassies and consulates

Both ambassadors and consuls are agents for a government appointed to attend to the interests of its citizens and commerce in another country. An ambassador is a diplomatic minister of the highest order and depending on whether an ambassador or consul has been appointed to a particular foreign city will depend whether the place where they carry on their business is referred to as an embassy or a consulate.

A foreign embassy or consulate in the UK will usually give you detailed advice and information on their country. Embassies are also authorised to issue visa and entry permits.

Activity 4.2.3

It is useful to know the addresses of the main embassies which you may need to contact.

Find out the embassy addresses for the following countries in London:

- Japan

- United States of America

- Saudi Arabia

- Australia.

Find out the address for the British Embassy in Japan, USA, Saudi Arabia and Australia.

Set out your answers on a fact sheet adding the addresses of any other embassies which you feel would be useful to you.

Other useful information to give to the traveller

1 The time differences of the countries to be visited (see Unit 1).

2 The languages spoken – a phrase book may be invaluable.

3 Driving restrictions and licence requirements of countries being visited.

4   Local banking hours.

5   Addresses of the nearest local embassies or consulates.

6   Any national holidays occuring during the visit and any restrictions these may impose.

UNIT
4

Work-related tasks

You are working for a firm of sportsware manufacturers and one of your duties is organising travel both home and abroad for all members of staff. The company has recently launched on to the market a set of golf clubs bearing the name of the company's consultant professional golfer – Gonzales Travasonni.

TASK ONE – Element 4.2

You receive the following memo:

M E M O R A N D U M

TO: You (Administrative Assistant)

FROM: Mike Flowers, Marketing Manager

DATE: 15 March 199–

TRAVASONNI GOLF CLUBS

From the available market research we believe that these new golf clubs should sell well in Germany, Brazil, USA, Japan and New Zealand.

I need to know the details of appropriate representatives for these countries in London. Their embassies or trade commissions will no doubt be a good starting point.

Would you find out the names, addresses and telephone numbers of the embassies or trade commissions of these countries together with any information which may help us in our export drive.

I would like this information as soon as possible please.

Thanks.

Mike Flowers

TASK TWO – Element 4.1

The sales director has said to you:

'I am planning a two-week trip to visit Japan and New Zealand in a couple of months' time. Please would you sort out my route, plane times from Heathrow and connecting flights. I also need to book a hotel for six nights in Tokyo and six nights in Wellington, New Zealand. Madge (my wife) will be accompanying me. So that I can reimburse the company for her travel and accommodation expenses please itemise these separately. We will be staying with my brother Brian in Auckland for two weeks before returning home.

'I need an itinerary including my hotel bookings. Also as I haven't got time would you type me out a quick letter to my brother Brian confirming that we expect to be seeing him at the beginning of June – the exact date I shall let him know later. Ask him if he has any good contacts or advice for selling golf clubs in New Zealand; he knows a lot of people out there.'

TASK THREE – Elements 4.1 and 4.2

Another member of the sales staff – Mamoon Rahman – is planning a business trip to Brazil. He knows little about the country apart from news coverage on television and the press. You have received the following memo from him.

```
M E M O R A N D U M

TO: You (Administrative Assistant)

FROM: Mamoon Rahman (Sales)

DATE: 18 March 199-

SOUTH AMERICA

I am trying to plan a sales trip to South America, in
particular to Brazil. I need a map of South America, to
know what language is spoken and the currency used. I
also need to know whether I require a vaccination
certificate or visa. If so, do you know how I may obtain
them?

In addition, the name and address of the British
Ambassador or Consul in Brazil. If there there is an
embassy it is likely to be in the main city, Brasilia.
Find out what weather I can expect if I go in June so
that I take the right clothes.

If there is anything else you can find out for me that
you think would be useful please let me have the
details.

Many thanks.

Mamoon Rahman
```

A couple of week's later, having found out the information for Mr Rahman, he sends you a second memo:

M E M O R A N D U M

TO: You (Administrative Assistant)

FROM: Mamoon Rahman (Sales)

DATE 1 April 199-

BRAZILIAN SALES TRIP

Many thanks for the information on Brazil.

The trip is going ahead and I'd like you to arrange a flight for me for 2 June 199-; if possible direct to Brazil without a change of plane.

I hope to stay in the main city Brasilia for about seven days. Please find me a good hotel there and write on my behalf, booking a single room with private bathroom for seven nights, giving dates and time of arrival, etc. Ask them to confirm the booking. Leave it on my desk ready for my signature.

No doubt you will prepare an itinerary for me. If you would include on it my train travel details from my home in Bury-St-Edmonds to Heathrow as usually I travel by car and have no idea of train times. I may be able to get someone to drive me out to the airport from our head office near Euston but if not how can I get to Heathrow from Euston?

Mamoon Rahman

TASK FOUR – Elements 4.1 and 4.2

You have received the following note from the chairman, Eric Peterson:

Susan (You)

A part-owner of this company and very old friend of mine from Holland, Frederick Van Husen, is staying with his wife in London. Two of the Directors and myself are meeting him at his hotel for a business meeting.

Please arrange to entertain Frederick's wife Gilda and show her London for the day while we discuss business.

I'll see you this morning at 11.00 am and you can give me some idea of your suggested programme for your day out tomorrow (Wednesday) with Mrs Van Husen. You will need to arrive at the Van Husen's hotel at about 10.00 am.

By the way, I know Gilda loves looking at the London shops and enjoys going to the theatre. She speaks English very well so that shouldn't be a problem. The company will pay for you both to have lunch out – please choose and book a good restaurant.

I know it would help Gilda if you could set out a table showing the comparative prices of goods. If you find out the Dutch currency and exchange rate and prepare a table to convert £ sterling into Dutch currency I know she would be delighted; she is always saying how confusing she finds currency conversion.

Eric Peterson

5 Preparing and producing documents

Main elements covered

5.1 Produce text from oral and written material using an alphanumeric keyboard

5.2 Present narrative, graphic and tabular information using an alphanumeric keyboard

5.3 Organise and arrange the copying, collating and binding of documents

Supplementary elements covered

2.2 Locate and abstract information from unspecified sources

2.3 Organise and present information in a variety of formats

Element 5.1 – Produce text from oral and written material using an alphanumeric keyboard

The work for this element may be carried out on either a typewriter or word processor. All transcripts produced for assessment for this unit must be 100 per cent accurate.

You will be expected to:

1 Produce approximately 1500 words in a 2½ hour working period from screen, manuscript and amended typescript;

2 Produce approximately 1200 words in a 2½ hour working period from pre-recorded speech (audio-typing); and

3 Compose approximately 300 words from brief notes and spoken instructions within a one-hour working period.

Corrections

To achieve competence in this unit your documents must be error-free. Apart from good keyboarding technique and *knowing* when you have produced an error the secret to submitting completely accurate work is good proof-reading skills.

Spellcheckers, which are available now on most good electronic typewriters and word-processing packages, mean that no minor spelling errors should appear in typed text any more. But remember it is still possible to be sloppy when using the spellchecker and to give the wrong command.

A spellchecker will not identify grammatical and punctuation errors. Always work towards improving your English skills. Have reference books to hand such as a good dictionery and *Roget's Thesaurus* as well as a book on English grammar, such as *Fowler's Modern English Usage*.

Activity 5.1.1

There are 15 words misspelt in the following group of 30 words:

useable; sensitive, temporary, accomodation, symptom, recieve, piece, seperate, rateable, plausable, pretense, tangible, labeling, priviledge, persue, niche, highten, illegible, honorary, deceit, acustom, aquire, agressive, apparent, champagne, cheif, wholy, whereabouts, unnecessary, survivor.

Find how long it takes for you to locate the mis-spelt ones and write out their correct spellings.

Another aid to producing error-free text is the memory facility and thin window display on many office electronic typewriters. By putting the text into delayed print the spelling and grammar may be checked for accuracy before being printed. However there are only a limited number of words visible at any one time and grammatical errors may not be apparent.

Word processors, on the other hand, are screen-based and give the operator the opportunity to check work before printing. Make sure the brightness on your screen is right for you so that any errors may be more readily recognised.

If you are working on equipment that has none of these features you will have to take much more care to try to minimise errors at source. You may have a correction ribbon on your typewriter. However, if errors are found and you have to use correcting paper make sure that the correction is well carried out and that the bits of paper do not fall into the machine! It is bad practice to use correcting fluid on an electronic typewriter.

For proof-reading skills see also Unit 6.

Activity 5.1.2

1 Timing yourself, find and mark the 10 errors in the text below. Type a corrected version of the text.

2 Timing yourself again, use a word-processing package with a spellchecker to key in, exactly, the text on page 80. Use the spellchecker facility to locate and amend the errors.

When you are away from the office it is sensable to arrange for someone to anwser your teliphone. Telling them where you may be locatted in an emergency and give them details of calls which may be recieved. If you are going to be away from the office for any length of time, say for three or for days, you could arrange for your callls to be roouted to the member of staff who is handling your work. When you return from your time away be sure to follow-up any messages that ave been left for you.

How long did each method take? Which was the quickest – you and a typewriter or the computer plus a spellchecker? Did the computer find all the errors?

When correcting typewritten or word-processed material for another member of staff to edit you should always use the standard correction signs.

FACT FINDER

Standard printers' correction signs are used to show amendments and alterations to text. Some of the most commonly used ones are shown below.

Standard correction signs

Sign (margin)	Meaning	Sign (text)	
l.c.	Lower case i.e. small letters	―	letter(s) to be altered, underlined
U.C. or CAPS	Upper case i.e. capital letters	―	letter(s) to be altered, underlined
∕	Delete	∕	through letter/word
// or N.P.	New paragraph	[	before first word
Run on	New paragraph not required	⌒	
⋋	Sign used to show where letter(s), word(s) punctuation mark etc. to be inserted	⋋	followed by text
#	Insert a space	⋋	
⌣	Close up space(s)	⌣	
trs	Transpose, i.e. change the order of letters, words or paragraphs	⊔⊓⊔	between text, some-times numbered
Stet	To remain as it was before	....	under words to be typed

Activity 5.1.3

Create a corrected version of the text below using a typewriter or word processor.

To achieve this element successfully it is necessary for the candidate to show a competent performance across a range of documents – letters envelopes, memos, forms labels, display material, appropriate copies. The text must contain both familiar and unfamiliar vocabulary with simple and complex grammatical structures.

The work may be carried out on a manual, electric typewriter or word processor. The production times specified in the Performance criteria include the usual pressures and interruptions, conflicts of demand and changes of priority experienced in a normal working environment.

Document presentation

If a piece of printed text is error-free but badly laid out it fails to create an impact or to encourage the receiver to take note of its content. In fact, very poor presentation of factual matter can lead to misunderstanding.

FACT FINDER

Standard typewriting theory, which includes some of the following, should be considered with regard to:

Display

Text display may be enhanced by the use of emboldening, double strike, italic, underlining or spacing capitals. Some typewriters and word-processing or desk top publishing packages are capable of giving a wide range of pitch and font.

Headings

When using different forms of heading, i.e. main heading, sub-heading, make sure that they are in different styles. For example:

BUSINESS ADMINISTRATION, NVQ LEVEL 3 (Main heading)

Unit 1 – Communication Systems (Sub-heading)

Margins

There are minimum margin values for top, bottom, left and right margins. Text should not be less than 1/2 inch from all sides of the paper. Generally, with a ragged right margin the left-hand margin should be wider than the right; with justified margins left and right margins should be equal.

Page numbers

The ability to number pages on a word processor automatically reduces effort. However, if you are putting in page numbers manually make sure you are consistent with your style.

Letter layout

There are three main styles of letter layout: fully blocked; blocked; and indented. Fully blocked is the more modern style. See the diagrams below:

Fully blocked style of letter layout

JENKINS & DOBBS LTD
Parsons Walk
CROYDON
CR2 8JK

Our ref MCA/NB

22 October 199-

For the attention of Mr Charles Green

Lister & Matthews Ltd
2 Fairview Road
Churchill Industrial Estate
TONBRIDGE
Kent
TN8 3CB

Dear Sirs

INSTALLATION OF OFFICE EQUIPMENT

Further to our telephone call to you on Friday 1 October 199-, we now enclose a copy of the invoice received by us from the plumber who came to remedy the damage caused to our water pipe by your workman.

The invoice has been paid by us. We therefore look forward to receiving your cheque for £98.34 in the very near future.

Yours faithfully
JENKINS & DOBBS

Michael Adams
Accountant

Enc

Blocked style of letter layout (similar to fully blocked but date and complimentary close offset towards right margin)

JENKINS & DOBBS LTD
Parsons Walk
CROYDON
CR2 8JK

Our ref MCA/NB   22 October 199-

For the attention of Mr Charles Green

Lister & Matthews Ltd
2 Fairview Road
Churchill Industrial Estate
TONBRIDGE
Kent
TN8 3CB

Dear Sirs

INSTALLATION OF OFFICE EQUIPMENT

Further to our telephone call to you on Friday
1 October 199-, we now enclose a copy of the invoice
received by us from the plumber who came to remedy the
damage caused to our water pipe by your workman.

The invoice has been paid by us. We therefore look
forward to receiving your cheque for £98.34 in the very
near future.

Yours faithfully
JENKINS & DOBBS

Michael Adams
Accountant

Enc

Semi-blocked (as for blocked but paragraphs are indented)

JENKINS & DOBBS LTD
Parsons Walk
CROYDON
CR2 8JK

Our ref MCA/NB   22 October 199-

For the attention of Mr Charles Green

Lister & Matthews Ltd
2 Fairview Road
Churchill Industrial Estate
TONBRIDGE
Kent
TN8 3CB

Dear Sirs

INSTALLATION OF OFFICE EQUIPMENT

> Further to our telephone call to you on Friday
1 October 199-, we now enclose a copy of the invoice
received by us from the plumber who came to remedy the
damage caused to our water pipe by your workman.

> The invoice has been paid by us. We therefore look
forward to receiving your cheque for £98.34 in the very
near future.

Yours faithfully
JENKINS & DOBBS

Michael Adams
Accountant

Enc

A company's house style may vary with regard to spacing, style of headings,
etc. and may not strictly adhere to one of the above layouts.

Punctuation

Open punctuation is discussed in Unit 6.

Spacing

Line spacing should be consistent with one clear line space between paragraphs.

There are various styles for spacing after punctuation. Again the main point to remember is to be consistent. A common style is one space after a comma and semi-colon, and two spaces after a full-stop, colon, question and exclamation marks.

Leave two clear line spaces after the main heading and one clear line space after sub-headings.

Tabulation

Basically, there should always be an equal number of spaces between columns.

The facility on word processors to centre, right or left align tabs or automatically create a decimal tab means that tabulated work on such equipment is far easier than on a manual or basic electronic typewriter.

Paper sizes

Although most electronic typewriters and word-processing software have facilities for aiding the operator when setting up complicated tabulated or displayed material it is still sometimes useful to know the international paper sizes to determine the best possible layout for a piece of work.

International paper sizes and details

Paper type	Size imperial (inches)	Size metric (mm)	Spaces across (Elite)	Spaces across (Pica)	Spaces down*
A4 Portrait	8¼ × 11¾	210 × 297	100	82	70
A4 Landscape	11¾ × 8¼	297 × 210	141	118	50
A5 Portrait	5 × 8¼	148 × 210	70	59	50
A5 Landscape	8¼ × 5	210 × 148	100	82	35
A6 Postcard	5 × 4	148 × 105	70	59	25

* 6 single vertical lines = 25 mm (1")

Elite = 12 characters = 25 mm (1") referred to as 12 pitch.

Pica = 10 characters = 25 mm (1") referred to as 10 pitch.

Elite and Pica are the most commonly used typefaces on electronic typewriters and computer printers.

Activity 5.1.4

You are working in the personnel department of an engineering company situated in North London. You have been asked to design and prepare a new application form from the details given below. Use your own discretion with display.

You have been told to prepare the form on a word processor in case any amendments are required.

Word processed application form

APPLICATION FORM

It is the policy of this company to provide equal opportunities in the fields of recruitment, training and promotion. All decisions in these areas will be made with regard to the requirements of the job and shall not be influenced by any consideration of race, colour, creed, ethnic or national origin, disabilities, age, gender, sexual orientation or marital status.

Interview and appointment procedures have been adopted so as to eliminate any possibilities of bias when considering applications.

POST APPLIED FOR   REFERENCE

PERSONAL DETAILS

NAME   MARITAL STATUS

PREVIOUS NAME (IF APPROPRIATE)

AGE   DATE OF BIRTH

ADDRESS   HOME TELEPHONE NO

Do you have a valid driving licence?

Medical Details

Do you suffer from any illness which may affect your work? (If 'Yes' please give details below.)

EDUCATION

Dates   School/College   Examinations taken   Results

CURRENT EMPLOYMENT

Appointment held   From

Name and Address of Employer

Salary and fringe benfits, e.g. car, luncheon vouchers, bonus

Brief outline of duties

PREVIOUS EMPLOYMENT (Most recent first)

Dates   Employer's name   Appointment held   Reason for
         and address   and brief details   leaving
                            of duties

SUPPORTING INFORMATION (you may give here any relevant information in support of your application)

REFERENCES

Please give details of two referees.

Name   Address

1

2

I declare that the information provided in this application is to the best of my knowledge correct.

Signed   Date

A few hours later you are handed this note:

Sorry, I forgot to give you this bit. Could you add it in an appropriate place. Thanks. Carol.

Addition to the application form

I would describe my ethnic origin* as (tick the appropriate box)

☐ BLACK   ☐ WHITE

☐ Afro-caribbean origin   ☐ European origin (including UK)

☐ African origin   ☐ Other (please specify)

☐ Asian origin

*Ethnic origin refers to a 'racial group' defined by the Race Relations Act 1976 as a group of persons described by reference to colour, race, nationality or ethnic origin.

My sex is:

☐ Male   ☐ Female

My marital status is

☐ Single   ☐ Married

Have you a disability which is relevant to your job description?

☐ Yes   ☐ No

If 'Yes' are you registered as disabled with the job centre? (Do you hold a green card?)

☐ Yes   ☐ No

Ergonomics and guidelines for use of keyboards and exposure to VDU screens

See Unit 10 for details.

Audio-transcription

The success of efficient audio work is dependent upon good dictation. It is essential that certain information is given to the audio-typist at specific points in the tape.

FACT FINDER

As an audio-typist you should expect the dictator to:

1 Announce their name, position and department.

2 Indicate priority items.

3 State the type of document and any special stationery required.

4 State how many copies of each document are required.

5 Give references.

6 Use the index scale slip on the dictating machine (if provided) to show the starting point of each document.

7 State when new paragraphs are required.

8 Dictate main punctuation marks.

9 Spell out names of people, places and unusual words.

10 Speak with a clear and steady voice.

For your part you should be familiar with how the audio-equipment operates. It is advisable to determine which is the most comfortable hearing equipment for *you* to use – a headset or earpiece. It can make a lot of difference and it is well worth the trouble to investigate an alternative method.

An audio-typist

Activity 5.1.5

(The following text will need to be put onto tape by either your tutor or a colleague.)

You are working in the administrative support section of a training and consultancy firm. One of the training officers has asked you to transcribe this text. He needs it urgently – it should not take you more than three-quarters of an hour.

Time yourself!

Text to be taped

FAMILIARISATION COURSE – COMPANY'S NEW WORD PROCESSING SYSTEM – INTRODUCTORY NOTES

Just in case some of you do not know who I am, let me introduce myself. I am Philip Hesquith and I am responsible for training in this company. Some of you may have joined the supervisory skills course that we ran a few weeks ago. This particular word-processing course will be running over ten weeks, for 1½ hours every Wednesday afternoon.

I am just going to give you a short introduction to the equipment and then I shall be handing you over to Ms Jenny Bianco who will take you through some practical tasks and also give you the advice and guidance you have requested. Please feel free to discuss with Ms Bianco any of the problems you are facing with the work that you have been doing so far. She has a very wide knowledge of the subject and is most keen to sort out any problems.

As you are aware, this company has fairly recently invested in a new computer network and some of you present have had some training on it, provided by the manufacturer. However, we understand everyone feels that more training and help is required before staff make full use of the new equipment. Also, some of the managers have felt it would be in everyone's best interests if they understood the work being carried out. They have therefore come along this afternoon to hear what is being said.

The printers we are using on the network are all laser printers. I understand that some of you have mastered this equipment very well and have been creating some good work. I'm sure Ms Bianco will be able to show you a few more things which will be new to you.

Our central memory is vast and is capable of storing all the data we need. In addition, you have a floppy disk drive at each work station so you will be keeping your own work on disks to be held by you. I know Ms Bianco will be talking to you later about disk housekeeping for those who have little knowledge of such procedures.

I'm now going to hand you over into the very capable hands of Ms Bianco. I'm sure you'll have a very informative and interesting afternoon.

Composing business documents

When composing business documents always use *simple* language. Think of the person receiving your communication. Will they appreciate its meaning? Take care with grammar and always check your work very carefully.

See also Unit 6.

FACT FINDER

Some hints on grammar

Always avoid:

1   Unnecessary repetition, for example, a new recent development.

2   Too many commas – commas are used less nowadays, but they are still necessary to convey the correct meaning or emphasis.

3   Jargon – this is a term for specialist words unlikely to be known by the majority of people, for example, using 'carpus' rather than 'wrist'.

4   Colloquialisms – these are words or expressions used in common conversation, for example, 'Where on earth'; 'Keep it under your hat'; 'Backs to the wall'; and 'don't', 'can't', etc.

5   Slang – these are words and phrases which are used in everyday speech. They are not generally accepted as standard English, but are widely understood, for example,'Slog' and 'Loo'.

6 Incomplete sentences, for example,'With reference to your letter of 14 November'.

7 Using words wrongly, for example, 'The animal had an incredulous (incredible) ability to resist all forms of attack'.

8 Placing prepositions at the end of sentences, for example, 'The person I gave it to.'

9 Split infinitives, for example, 'She tried to hastily beat a retreat' should be changed to 'She tried hastily to beat a retreat' or 'She tried to beat a hasty retreat'.

10 Inconsistency with tenses, for example, 'I *shall* be happy if you *would*' should be changed to 'I *should* be happy if you *would*'.

Activity 5.1.6

The letter below needs amending! You may understand the message it is trying to convey but it is written in very poor English. Write out a corrected version.

```
Dear Mr Jones

Further to my previous letter of 18 November.

I will be pleased if you should let me have your cheque
for £300.00 promptly at your convenience.

We have our backs to the wall in this company and I can
see no light at the end of the tunnel to the problems I
am facing up to.

Please don't make me seek justice in the courts. But if
you can't let me have my lolly quickly our business
friendship will be finally concluded.

Yours sincerely
```

Commonly mis-used words

Some people constantly have problems with which word of a pair of words to use in a particular situation.

Examples of good practice:

Should and **would**

'**I should** be glad if you **would** let me know your answer by the end of next week.'

Neither and **nor**

'**Neither** the agenda **nor** the notice of the meeting gave any indication of the trouble that occurred.'

Either and **or**

'We can **either** go by train **or** by car to the conference.'

Accept and **except**

'I am happy to **accept** your offer of help.'

'All the items were faulty **except** the ones bought today.'

Principle and **principal**

'She had very high **principles** and had never been known not to tell the truth.'

'The **principal** beneficiary under his will was his wife.'

Bought and **brought**

'She **bought** a very large turkey for £6.00.'

'He **brought** several of his friends with him.'

Stationery and **stationary**

'The stock of **stationery** was very low.'

'The car was **stationary** at the traffic lights.'

Activity 5.1.7

In the following paragraphs check the use of words and write out a corrected version.

The Principle parked her car outside the shop and went and brought some stationary for her dancing school. They cost a great deal of money but as it was a principal of hers not to have credit she paid in cash.

She had wanted to find out whether it would have any affect on the overall bill if she brought in bulk. However neither the salesgirl or the manager were able to give her full details.

Care of electronic equipment

See Unit 1 for details.

Element 5.2 – Present narrative, graphic and tabular information using an alphanumeric keyboard

If you are involved in keying in and processing personal details on a computer you should be aware of the main provisions of the Data Protection Act 1984. The Act was passed to give protection to the public from the adverse effects of incorrect information which may be stored about individuals on computer.

FACT FINDER

The Data Protection Act 1984

Basically, the Act provides for individuals to have access to data about themselves for checking. If the information is incorrect they may have it deleted or amended as appropriate. In some cases, compensation may be awarded where an individual has suffered loss or damage due to inaccurate data.

Organisations involved in using data-processing equipment are required to register with the Data Protection Registrar and data stored by these organisations is vetted for approval by the Registrar. A list of such organisations, together with details of the type of data they hold, is available at major public libraries.

See also Unit 2.

Sources of information

The following describes one of the performance criteria for this element:

'Error-free documents of approximately 300 words are compiled from a variety of sources and produced in a one-hour working period.'

There are many sources of information available for the office as follows:

1 There are the various directories already mentioned – Telephone, Yellow Pages, facsimile and telex directories.

2 Basic reference books for travel – *ABC Guides*, the *AA* and *RAC handbooks*.

3 General reference books useful in the office – *Croner's Office Companion*, and *Whitaker's Almanack*.

4 Information on companies – *Stock Exchange Yearbook*, *UK Kompass*.

5 English reference books – dictionaries, *Roget's Thesaurus*, *Fowler's Modern English Usage*.

6 Specialist reference books – *Banker's Almanac and Yearbook, Municipal Yearbook.*

7 Office magazines – *Office Equipment News* and *Mind Your Own Business.*

Other sources of information include government departments, local authority offices, banks and building societies, and trade or professional associations.

See also Unit 1.

Activity 5.2.1

You are working in an estate agents who are expanding their operations to the continent.

You have been asked to find out the answer to the following questions. Write down your answer giving the source of your information.

1 Where is the headquarters of the European Community?

2 What are the frequency of planes to Copenhagen from Birmingham Airport? Which airlines operate this route?

3 What is the approximate distance in miles and kilometres between Carnac on the Brittany coast to Barcelona in Spain?

4 What are the postal charges on letters and small packets to Italy?

Viewdata

Viewdata is an on-screen, interactive information service available to the public and the business community.

Prestel is the public viewdata service run by British Telecom. There are private viewdata services for the specialist user such as *Travicom* used by travel agents.

To use a viewdata service it is necessary to rent or buy special equipment and to have the use of a telephone line. The *Prestel* service brings the user into contact with over a quarter of a million pages or screens of information from a central database. For some information a charge will be made whilst other pages can be accessed free of charge.

Institutions such as the Stock Exchange, *Good Food Guide* and the English Tourist Board provide information on a wide range of subjects, such as stock market prices, travel, current affairs and government statistics. The information providers regularly update their information.

The use of a keyboard or pad with the equipment provides a two-way interaction between the customer and computer database. It is therefore possible to order goods or book travel through the system.

To prevent misuse of such a system a password is usually incorporated into the database access procedure.

Activity 5.2.2

1 Observe the use of a viewdata terminal and find out what special facilities are being used by the operator.

2 Use a viewdata or teletext terminal (similar in some respects to viewdata but *not* interactive) to appreciate how different pages of information are brought to the screen.

Element 5.3 – Organise and arrange the copying, collating and binding of documents

As an office worker involved in photocopying a wide range of documents it is useful to know the position regarding copyright of printed material.

FACT FINDER

Copyright guidelines

Office workers need to be aware of the copyright laws. The recent Copyright, Designs and Patents Regulations are intended to tighten up the law as laid down in the 1956 Copyright Act.

Legally, the author of a piece of work is the copyright owner and s/he has the right to transfer this ownership to another person, such as a publisher. However, should the author have created the work whilst in employment, the employer may be the owner of the copyright unless there is an agreement to the contrary.

Copyright of a work exists from the moment of its existence and it is not necessary for the work to be published for it to be protected by copyright. No formal registration is necessary.

Anyone who then copies material and uses it for their own use may be in breach of copyright and legal action could be taken against them.

Some establishments purchase copyright waivers to allow them to copy certain material. In other situations copying of material is allowed after a certain date. Always check – be sure of the position *before* you copy material.

Activity 5.3.1

Investigate the copyright situation at your place of work or study.

1 Is there any material produced for or by the company which is copyright classified?

2 Has the company purchased any copyright waivers?

3 Has the company been given permission to use copyright material?

Binding equipment

There is a wide variety of binding equipment now on the market. Some equipment uses heat whilst other machines use plastic or wire spines to bind the pages together.

Activity 5.3.2

Collate all the work produced by you for the different units. Photocopy the frontispiece prepared under Activity 2.3.3 to allow one per unit of work. Fasten all the papers together with available binding equipment.

Reprographic equipment

Copiers

There is a vast range of copiers available to the business community. The use of microchip technology has brought about the 'intelligent' copier which allows the document to be copied, processed, transmitted to distant locations or stored for future use.

The facilities available on a copier may include:

- reduction and enlargement of original;

- finishing facilities, i.e. collating, binding/stapling;

- reproduction in colour;

- use of credit cards to control the use of the copier;

- preparation of overhead transparencies and offset plates.

The price of copiers range from a few hundred pounds for a simple desktop model to many thousands for those providing a full range of 'extra' facilities.

Offset duplicators

Many organisations still use an offset duplicator to produce such items as their letterheads and advertising brochures. This method is generally used because of the high quality of copy achievable and the relatively cheap method of reproducing colour and long runs.

Activity 5.3.3

1 Investigate the reprographic methods in use at your place of work or study. Find out approximately how many copies are produced on the equipment each week and the approximate price per copy.

2 What guidelines would you give to a new junior in the office to ensure that s/he does not waste copy paper and always produces work of a good standard?.

Equipment faults

For details see Unit 1.

UNIT
5

Work-related tasks

You are working for the firm of Allen Nicholls Ltd who are an engineering company operating in North London. You are an administrative assistant in the personnel and training department and work for James Plummer, the personnel and training manager, as well as for other members of the personnel team.

You have the following tasks to complete.

TASK ONE – Elements 5.1 and 5.2

Chris

Some typing for you. We have interviews for an Office Manager tomorrow and we haven't got a list of those on the short list. Could you do this for me as priority please.

Thanks. Jim.

PS Would you treat this list as confidential please – not all employers know that these individuals are coming here for interview.

```
POST OF OFFICE MANAGER
Short list of applicants:

Jane ANDREWS
Flat 2, 23 Jackson Street, Islington, London.

Peter KAY
912 Dorking Road, Ealing, London.

Lisa CHAN
12 West Road, Wembley, Middlesex.

Kulbinder SANDHU
90 Acacia Avenue, Northwick Park, Middlesex.

Chris MAUNDER
65 Minster Close, Camden, London.
```

TASK TWO – Elements 5.1, 5.2 and 5.3

Chris

The minutes as usual please. Hope you can read my scribble! Please add an action column. (*See Unit 8.*)

Jim

Minutes of the Health & Safety Committee Meeting held on Wednesday 17 June 199- at 2.00 pm in the Board Room

Present: K L Kildoon (Chairperson), M Raison, J Shah,
B Dunn, A Mucklewaite, J Plummer (Secretary)

MINUTES OF PREVIOUS MEETING:

The minutes of the meeting held on Wednesday 13 May 199- had been distributed to all members of the committee. An amendment under Item (5) the date of the Business Security Conference was changed to 18 September 199-. The minutes were then approved and signed by the Chairperson.

MATTERS ARISING FROM MINUTES

Item 3 – Repairs

It was stated that the unsafe floor covering in the entrance to Block 2 had now been repaired and should not cause any more problems. The problems with ventilation in the offices were however causing more difficulty. An inspection had been made after the last work had been completed but it was considered that the level of ventilation was still inadequate.

Item 5 – Safety Conference

The arrangements for the Business Security Conference were well under way. It was to be held on Markham's premises and it was expected that there would be many visitors from local commerce and industry.

There were to be two main speakers during the afternoon whilst the morning would be taken up with demonstrations of security equipment and devices. There would be representatives on hand to give advice.

The Chairman, Mark Nicholls would introduce the afternoon speakers. It would be held in the Board Room with a restriction that they were by 'invitation only'.

Members of the press had been invited to attend and it was agreed that M Raison should be in charge of them.

FIRST AID TRAINING

The second session of First Aid Training was to commence at the beginning of September. It would be held between 4.00 pm to 5.30 pm on Thursdays for 12 weeks. There would be six members of staff attending the programme which when they had all successfully completed the course would mean that the company would be well staffed with professionally qualified First Aiders.

VDU HEALTH CONCERN

It was reported that several members of the female staff had approached the management expressing their concern at the lack of knowledge on the effects of radiation from VDUs on unborn children. They asked if something could be done about the situation.

During a long discussion it was stated that there was no proof that there were any harmful effects from VDUs but in the meantime it was agreed that:

a) negotiations should commence between the Union and Management to bring in arrangements whereby pregnant women could be given alternative work if they so wished and

b) a working party be set up to look at the general conditions of staff working with VDUs and that guidelines should be prepared to ensure that the health and well-being of staff was not being damaged in any way.

VACANCY ON COMMITTEE

It was stated that due to the retirement of Colin Kingsley there was a vacancy on the Committee. Mr Kingsley represented the Workshop and it was agreed that the Chairperson should write to members in that section asking for a volunteer to sit on the Committee. If there was more than one nominee then a vote would need to be taken.

ANY OTHER BUSINESS

It was suggested that there should be a company safety competition. It was necessary to raise the awareness of all members of staff to the need for good health and safety procedures at all times. After a discussion it was agreed that the following proposal should be put to Management:

A company competition be run to find the best health and safety logo for the company. The winning entry would be added to all documents of the company to ensure that good health and safety practices were always followed.

DATE AND TIME OF NEXT MEETING

The next meeting would be held on Wednesday 15 July 199- at 2.00 pm in the Board Room.

Signature and date lines as usual please.

TASK THREE – Elements 5.1 and 5.2

You found the following note on your desk when you arrived for work this morning.

```
Chris

We are trying to put together a staff handbook. It will
have information about staff, the company structure and
facilities offered by the company. It will also have
details on such matters as the restaurant, telephone
system, reception and visitors, meeting rooms, salaries,
petty cash, etc.

These are just notes on the handbook so put them into
proper sentences. Make sure the whole is clear and
understandable by all. The Chairman has already prepared
the introduction. Other sections are to follow.

Thanks.   Jim

PS     So far I've only done notes on the three sections.
I would like all sections to be about 70/75 words each.
```

Petty cash

Petty cash only for small items like taxi fares, emergencies. Give the procedure about obtaining a VAT receipt (see Unit 9). The limit on a petty cash voucher is £20.00. Mention about authorisation.

Petty cash is only paid out in the morning between 10-12 noon. Say that the Assistant to the Accounts Manager is the Petty Cashier. His name is Ryan Smith.

Restaurant

Say the restaurant is mainly for staff use. Visitors may use the facility provided they first of all contact Mrs Banda the Restaurant Manager. Give the hours of opening together with prices for basic meals – breakfast, lunch and tea. Give some information on the other food that may be bought in the restaurant. Mention about alcohol – only allowed for special business lunches. You could mention that tea and coffee may be ordered and delivered to offices provided sufficient notice is given.

Sick leave

Say that staff must always call in to the Company as early as possible if they are going to be off sick. If you are away over three days you will need to fill in a self-certification form, if away for over a week need a doctor's certificate (full details in Conditions of Service Booklet). Add about the location of the Sick Room being on the Fifth floor in Room 51.

TASK FOUR – Element 5.1

Chris

Would you please make the following amendments to our standard letter confirming employment. If we could put this on disk it would be very useful as then we would be able to amend it easily in the future.

Thanks. Jim

Dear ~~With reference to~~

~~Further to~~ your recent interview I am ~~able~~ to confirm my offer of the appointment as _____ with effect from _____ .

The appointment is subject to the Conditions of Service a copy of which is attached. Your commencing salary is _____ from which there will be a deduction in respect of the Company's ~~Superannuation~~ Scheme. Please let me have your written acceptance of this appointment as soon possible.

Yours sincerely

James Plummer

Personnel Manager

Enc

Processing correspondence

Main elements covered

6.1   Identify and respond to correspondence for own action

Supplementary elements covered

2.2   Locate and abstract information from unspecified sources

2.2   Organise and present information in a variety of formats

5.1   Produce text from oral and written material using an alphanumeric
keyboard

Element 6.1 – Identify and respond to correspondence for own action

Business correspondence is one of the main means of communication between
business organisations and their contacts. In this unit 'correspondence' refers to
the whole range of written communication – letters, memos, circulars, enquiries,
quotations, invoices, statements, advertisements, notices and invitations.

Identifying correspondence for own action

As your career develops you may find a higher proportion of your employer's
correspondence is delegated to you. In some instances, whole areas of work may
be placed directly under your control and it will be your responsibility to initiate
and respond to correspondence as necessary.

The following will help you ensure that you give an efficient and correct
response to correspondence received:

1   A good knowledge of your company's organisational structure and the
various job titles of staff should be an asset in determining any
correspondence which should be 'passed on' for action.

2   Prioritise correspondence. It is important that correspondence once identified
as requiring *your* attention is dealt with promptly and correctly.

3   Keeping a file of standard letters is useful and initially will enable you to
overcome any problems you may have in obtaining the right tone and style for
your letters.

4   An appropriate follow-up file or similar would also be helpful in ensuring no replies are forgotten or held up.

When prioritising your correspondence, similar questions to those used to determine your own work schedule and what should be done first (see Unit 7, Element 7.2) need to be asked.

What are the likely effects of responding or not responding to the correspondence on:

1   The finances of the company?

2   The company's image/good relations with its customers and members of staff?

3   Your image/good relationship with the company's customers and other members of staff?

Activity 6.1.1

It is Friday and you are working for a firm of builders merchants. Due to staff sickness and holidays your working life is exceptionally busy. However, you have set up various aids to help you deal with an extra workload. These are the tasks you have to deal with. Discuss the situation and state which items you would deal with first and why:

1   A circular letter to potential customers needs to be composed and 200 copies photocopied and posted. The letter is about a special window offer to commence in two weeks' time.

2   There have been several telephone enquiries during the morning which require investigating and a quotation sent out.

3   Ten letters need to be sent out to clients requesting payment of their overdue accounts.

4   Twenty invoices need to be checked before being posted.

5   One hundred invitations to a 'Cheese & Wine' must be sent out to customers. The event takes place in four weeks.

Note: You have no other member of staff to whom you can delegate and you are on holiday for two weeks from next Monday.

Responding to correspondence for own action

As an administrative assistant you may frequently be called upon to compose correspondence and always remember that any such communication presents an image of your company. If your work is badly put together the recipient will get a poor impression of the company and its products.

FACT
FINDER

Basic rules to remember

1 **Presentation**. The layout of the correspondence should conform to your company's house style and be printed on appropriately headed paper. It should not contain printing or grammatical errors.

2 **Accuracy**. All facts in the correspondence should be correct especially such items as dates, times, amounts of money, etc.

3 **Clarity.** The reader should easily understand the meaning of the correspondence and be confident that any action taken is correct. Ambiguity may result in the wrong action being put into effect.

4 **Conciseness.** The correspondence should keep to the point and be brief without being abrupt or vague.

5 **Consistency.** Always make sure that one piece of information in one part of the correspondence is not contradicted by a comment in another part. Such errors lead to confusion.

6 **Style.** When composing correspondence for signature by another individual it is advisable to adapt to that person's style of writing. When composing your own correspondence you are allowed to create and use your own style. However there is no need to use a special vocabulary; everyday words are far more likely to be understood.

7 **Misrepresentation.** Be very careful not to involve you or your company in any legal battle. Never exaggerate about the company's products or services. Do not say when describing an item of furniture being sold that it is antique when in fact it is reproduction nor that your firm offers a 24-hour service when in fact it closes down between 10.00 pm and 6.00 am. You could say that the item of furniture is one of the most attractive of its type or that the service offered by your company is the finest in the area. But take care!

8 **Tact.** Always be tactful whether you are dealing with a complaint from a customer or a problem with another member of staff.

9 **Initial preparation.** When you first start to compose your own business correspondence it is helpful if you first list all the points you wish to make in logical order. You should certainly make sure you have all the facts to hand and any previous correspondence which is relevant.

10 Punctuation. Use the same style of punctuation throughout your correspondence. If you are using open punctuation remember:

a) Grammatical punctuation must still be used.

b) When typing a business letter *no* punctuation at all is inserted in the reference, date, name and address of the addressee, salutation or following the complimentary close. When addressing an envelope *no* punctuation is inserted. Examples of the two styles are:

Open punctuation:	17 May 1991
Full punctuation:	17th May, 1991,
Open punctuation:	Mr R Johnson
	592 Barnwood Road
	GLOUCESTER
	GL1 6FG
Full Punctuation:	Mr. R. Johnson,
	592, Barnwood Road,
	GLOUCESTER.
	GL1 6FG

c) In continuous matter where a name and address 'run on' commas are inserted.

Example: Mr R Johnson, 592 Barnwood Road, Gloucester.

d) When an abbreviation ends in a full stop, the full stop is omitted and replaced by a space.

For example, P.O.Box would be P O Box.

e) Where abbreviations consist of two or more letters with full stops after each letter, the full stops are omitted and no space is left between the letters. A space is left after each group of letters.

Examples:

Open punctuation: Mrs A Hill BA JP

Full punctuation: Mrs. A. Hill, B.A., J.P.

f) *Never* insert full stops in the 24-hour clock.

Example: 1300 hours

However the 12-hour clock requires a full stop even when open punctuation is used.

Example: 1.00 pm

Activity 6.1.2

You are working at an electronics wholesale business. You have been asked to write a memo to all staff asking for their assistance and vigilance in combating the petty pilfering that appears to be going on. The recent stock-taking showed discrepancies (see Unit 9 if you require some information on stock-taking).

Business letters

Although keeping to your company's house style when setting out business letters there are specific features you should consider.

FACT FINDER

Salutation

The salutation should always agree with the name and address of the addressee. If your letter is addressed to the personnel manager of a particular company your letter should begin with 'Dear Sir' *not* 'Dear Sirs'. Likewise, if a letter is addressed to an individual it should begin 'Dear Mr Jones'.

When writing a business letter it is important to use the correct form of address. Some basic rules are as follows:

1 Courtesy titles, for example, Mr, Sir, Miss should always be used on both the letter and envelope.

2 Use Mr *or* Esq when writing to a male person. Be consistent, do not use both. Esq is now rarely used.

3 Sir, Rev or Dr replaces Mr or Esq.

4 Letters after a person's name must be arranged in order of importance as follows:

    a) decorations and honours, for example, VC;
    b) Royal appointments, for example, JP;
    c) University degrees, for example, BA;
    d) letters other than university degrees denoting medical qualifications, for example, FRCS;
    e) membership of professional institutions, for example, FRS;
    f) letters indicating an appointment or office, for example, MP.

Titles

When addressing letters to people overseas it may be difficult to be certain that you are following the correct format. Chambers of Commerce may be able to help you or you could contact the embassy of the country concerned.

The table below shows the equivalent way to address individuals in some other European languages:

English	Mr	Mrs	Miss
French	Monsieur	Madame	Mademoiselle
German	Herr	Frau	Fräulein
Italian	Signor	Signora	Signorina
Spanish	Señor	Señora	Señorita

The salutation for these languages are:

French:	Monsieur
	Madame
	Mademoiselle
German:	Sehr geehrter Herr
	Sehr geehrte Frau
	Sehr geehrtes Fräulein
Italian:	Gentilissimo Signor or Egregio Signor
	Distinta Signora
	Esimia Signorina
Spanish:	Muy Señor Mio
	Muy Estimada Señora
	Muy Distinguida Señorita

Headings

A heading to a letter is often the first item to catch the reader's eye. It immediately lets the reader know the main purpose of the letter. Use concise, appropriate headings both for the benefit of the recipient and to aid filing.

Paragraphs

Most business letters have three parts:

1 An opening paragraph which is usually an acknowledgement of an incoming letter or a telephone conversation. Such a paragraph may read:

'Thank you for your letter of 23 July 199-.'
or
'With reference to the Statement of Account received from you today ...'
or
'We were sorry to hear from your letter of 10 October 199- that you are not satisfied with the condition of the goods delivered under Order ref 1234.'
or
'Further to our recent telephone conversation we are pleased to confirm that ...'
or
'Following our telephone conversation of 23 July 199- we are pleased to confirm that ...'

2 The main body of the letter. As with any communication this should be adequately paragraphed and displayed so that it can be easily read. If several subjects are discussed further headings should be used.

3 A closing paragraph. Some letters do not require a closing paragraph but it is useful to write one so that the reader is left in no doubt what the next stage in the correspondence should be. Such a paragraph may be:

'We look forward to hearing from you.'
or
'If there is any further information or help you require please do not hesitate to contact us again at the above address or on telephone number ...'
or
'Thank you for your assistance.'

The complimentary close

The usual forms are 'Yours sincerely' and 'Yours faithfully' with 'Yours truly' being used very occasionally by some executives. The form used should agree with the salutation. Generally, 'Dear Sir' is followed by 'Yours faithfully' and 'Dear Mr Jones' is followed by 'Yours sincerely'. 'Yours truly' is slightly less formal than 'Yours faithfully'.

If you are going to sign the letter in your executive's absence it is usual to type 'Dictated by Mr Jones and signed in his absence'. Alternatively, you can preface the name of the sender with the letters 'pp' – standing for *per procurationem* – if you have been authorised to do so.

With other European languages the complimentary close is as follows:

France	Avec mes meilleurs sentiments
German	Mit Freundlichem Gruss
Italian	Cordiali saluti
Spanish	le saluda atentamente.

Activity 6.1.3

1 Locate an appropriate reference book (for example, Debretts) which will give you detailed information on the correct way to address titled individuals.

   From this reference book find out the correct way to address a letter to the following:

   a) The Archbishop of Canterbury
   b) The Governor General of Australia
   c) The Mayor of the nearest town to where you live
   d) Your local MP.
   e) The Mayor of Lille, France.

2 Locate a reference book which will give you the full wording of the abbreviations such as VC, JP, BA, FRCS, FRS and MP.

Proof-reading

Proof-reading can be somewhat tiresome and unproductive when you are very busy. However, if a valued customer receives several pages of well presented material only to find that there are several errors in the text and figure work, this could lead to loss of confidence in the company and even in extreme circumstances to loss of business.

As stated in Unit 5, one advantage of modern technology has been the electronic spellchecker. Whilst such a program will not locate all errors, especially if a word or a whole line has been missed out, it will certainly find a high proportion of them. Make sure if you have one on your typewriter or computer that you use it as a matter of routine. But do not forget headings, they are easily missed.

You should consciously aim to improve your proof-reading technique. Be on the look-out for common errors. The *is* for *if* and *has* instead of *as* type of error may be overlooked when checking and are not shown up as errors by spellcheckers. Grammatical errors, such as changing tenses in the middle of a paragraph or incorrect punctuation, will also not be found by a spellchecker.

It may be difficult to check the text on some VDU screens if the brightness and contrast has not been adjusted to suit you. Always check these before you start working.

Activity 6.1.4

Check the following paragraph for errors and type out a corrected copy:

BLACK & SON – ESTABLISHED FIRM OF SHOP-FITTERS – SINCE 1805

This firm founded in 1850 by the Great Grandfather of the present owner Benny Black. They are renowned for their modern approach to shop-fitting with their use of innovative and colourful materials. Several other members of the Slack family work in the business. Their is Angela Black, wife of Benny, who is in charge of financial maters. Then there is Jim, the younger brother of Benny, who likes to think that he is the one how keeps the business going. He is the entrapreneurial type always wanting to set up new projects and use new products. Lastley there is Jane the daughter of Angela and Benny. She was very plane as a child but know she is a fashionable and very glamourous Sales Consultant for the family busness.

Proof-reading numbers is very tiring and requires a great deal of concentration. Spellcheckers are of no use in such circumstances. It is useful, if you have a large amount of figure work to check, to have another member of staff assist you and for the numbers to be read out loud.

Activity 6.1.5

A: Sales figures from 1985-90

		Region		
Year	South	West	North	East
1985	123,452	342,987	210,327	318,642
1986	201,912	352,999	231,387	318,980
1987	211,435	343,121	254,786	319,922
1988	209,324	376,119	287,652	260,312
1989	219,245	389,722	297,023	287,098
1990	220,876	428,134	287,549	276,120

B: Sales figures from 1985-90

		Region		
Year	South	West	North	East
1985	123,452	342,987	210,827	318,662
1986	201,912	352,999	251,387	318,980
1987	201,435	345,121	254,786	318,922
1988	209,314	376,719	287,652	260,312
1989	219,245	389,722	297,028	287,998
1990	220,856	418,134	287,549	276,130

You have been handed the above two sets of figures (A and B) on separate sheets of paper. Set A is the original, correct version which has been prepared on a typewriter. Set B has been prepared on computer but mistakes have been made. Circle the mistakes with a pencil and produce a correct copy on a computer.

UNIT

6

Work-related tasks

You are working in a branch office of The Golden Travel Company and you deal with all correspondence relating to travel in the United Kingdom. Another member of staff deals with foreign travel.

TASK ONE – Element 6.1

You have received some complaints over the telephone from clients who went on a recent coach trip to the Cotswolds that had been organised by your company.

They complained that the coach was unheated and dirty, and although there should have been fresh drinking water and soft drinks available on the coach this was not the case. Furthermore, the driver refused to stop on the way to let them buy any. They have all asked for a refund.

You have investigated the situation and found that the complaint is justified. You have also spoken to the branch manager who has offered to reimburse these clients 50 per cent of what they paid for the trip.

Write a letter informing these clients of the offer.

Their names are:

- Mrs Janet Harris, 45 Westbourne Road, Stanmore

- Mrs Iris Turner, 6 High Way, Pinner.

TASK TWO – Element 6.1

You have the following letter on your desk, together with a couple of invoices and a circular about a special offer on office furniture. State how you would deal with these items.

```
                                        29 Jackson Street
                                        Harrow
                                        Middlesex
The Golden Travel Company
10 The High Street                      4 August 199-
Kenton
Middlesex

Dear Sirs

Please would you send me particulars about any package
tours to Norway. I would like to go there for my summer
holidays during the month of September.

I look forward to hearing from you.

Yours sincerely


Margaret Woodhouse
```

You also have the following invitation on your desk from the managing director. Deal with appropriately.

```
M E M O R A N D U M

TO: All Branch Staff

FROM: Ted Jackson (Managing Director)

DATE: 5 August 199-

ANNUAL GOLDEN TRAVEL BBQ

You may have already heard that the Annual Golden Travel
BBQ is to be held on Friday 6 September 1992 at the
Westway Leisure Park, Croydon. The Guildford Branch will
be acting as hosts this year and I hope we shall all
have a great time.

The BBQ is scheduled to start at 6.0 pm. A coach will
leave Head Office at 4.30 pm for those requiring
transport and it will return you to base at about
midnight. Please leave your name with my secretary if
you want to take advantage of this facility.

Please let my secretary know by 1 September if you are
able to come along.

Ted Jackson
```

TASK THREE – Element 6.1

It is Friday 16 August and the branch manager has passed the following half-prepared letter to you. It was written by a temporary assistant who has now gone on sick leave.

Attached to the letter is a note which reads:

Please write to Mr Houston and inform him that the cost of the holiday would be £135.00 each for him and his wife. This includes coach travel and a week's accommodation, half board, at the Seagull Guest House, Torquay. Apologise for the problems with his booking and tell him that in view of the upset we would like to give him a 15 per cent reduction on his full bill should he wish to confirm his reservation. Would you tell him exactly what that would be, so that there is no misunderstanding.

Also add a paragraph about Golden Travel always being available to give help and advice with holidays and for clients to contact us whenever they wish. In addition, you need to add that the office will be closed over the Bank holiday on both Monday and Tuesday, the 26 and 27 August, although we will be open between 9.00 am and 5.00 pm on Saturday 24 August.

Many thanks

Jack

The half-prepared letter is as follows:

THE GOLDEN TRAVEL COMPANY
10 The High Street
Kenton
Middlesex

13 August 199-

Mr J Houston
23 Windward Way
Northwood Park
Middlesex

Dear Mr Houston

Thank you for your letter of 10 August 199- informing us that you had booked a holiday with us to Torquay for a week during September but that since April you have not heard a word from us.

Your tickets are in the office ...

TASK FOUR – Element 6.1

You have received the following memo. Find out the information requested
and give your reply in a memo.

```
M E M O R A D U M


TO: You


FROM: J Grade (Branch Manager)


DATE: 20 August 1992


DOCKLANDS LIGHT RAILWAY

The office has had a number of people enquiring about
the Docklands Light Railway. With the development going
on in the area, I feel it would be useful to have
information on the system to enable the company to give
a better service to our customers.

Would you find out all you can about this service and
give me the facts in writing as soon as possible.

Many thanks.
```

TASK FIVE – Element 6.1

You also have the quotation below which has been handed to you with the
following note.

```
Please calculate the figures for the following quotation
as a matter of urgency and type it up. The request came
through several days ago and Miss Satchi is enquiring
when it will be ready. Date it 15 August and add that a
5 per cent discount will be given if full payment is
received before the end of August. Give the discounted
total as well.

Thanks

Jack

21/8/9-
```

For: Miss B Satchi of 231 Kingswood Lane, Kenton, Middlesex

In reply to your enquiry of 8 August 199- we have pleasure in quoting the following:

> Hire of Golden Travel Mini Bus plus driver to transfer eight persons from 231 Kingswood Lane, Kenton to Heathrow Airport Terminal 3 on Saturday 22 September 199- at £8.75 per person.

Total Cost £

> Hire of Golden Travel Mini Bus plus driver to transfer 12 persons from Heathrow Airport Terminal 3 to 231 Kingswood Lane, Kenton on Saturday 6 October 199- at £8.75 per person.

Total Cost £

We look forward to receiving your instructions which will receive our prompt attention.

Organising work schedules

Main elements covered

7.1 Manage appointments

7.2 Organise own work schedule

Supplementary elements covered

2.1 Use and develop manual and computerised filing systems

Element 7.1 – Manage appointments

Appointments are made for a whole range of situations – meetings, interviews, attendance at conferences and seminars are but a few. A busy schedule requires a well-kept record of where you or your employer should be at any particular time.

Most office staff will use a diary to schedule their appointments. There is a wide choice of diaries on the market and it is easier if you and your employer have the same style of diary.

Some people prefer a traditional diary, others prefer a more modern electronic one. Some office workers may prefer to have one for appointments and one for work to be done. A few diaries have the time printed off in half- or one-hour blocks. If not it is advisable to leave spaces so that appointments may be entered in correct sequence.

**FACT
FINDER**

When making appointments, whether for yourself or for your employer, there are several rules you should always follow.

1 *Never* double-book.

2 Always be generous with the length of time given to an appointment. Leave blocks of uncommitted time during the day.

3 Check the location of an appointment and take into account any travelling time involved.

4 Check for any other critical work that day, for example, a meeting or report to be submitted.

5 Obtain *full* information on the appointment – name, job title, reason for appointment and telephone number for prior contact in case this is required (see also point 15 below).

6 Record the 'finish time' if known.

7 Always confirm an appointment made on the telephone in writing.

8 If arranging an appointment for another individual obtain agreement on arrangements made as soon as possible and then confirm the appointment with the third party in writing.

9 You should always check your employer's diary before committing her/him to any activity. Amendments may have been made to original entries.

10 Be sure to warn your employer about appointments in plenty of time and have all necessary files and papers to hand.

11 It is good practice to have a briefing with your employer for the next day's business either in the late afternoon or first thing in the morning.

12 If appropriate, type up an appointments list for each day, giving a copy to reception.

13 Use codes/symbols to note priority or provisional appointments.

14 If using a traditional diary use pencil in case items require alteration.

15 When confirming appointments for visitors to your company it is sometimes helpful to give brief directions to your location. If someone is coming by car it is useful for them to receive advice on parking. You may possibly need to reserve a parking space for the visitor.

Similarly, if a visitor is arriving by rail or plane s/he needs to know whether they are being met and if so how that person may be identified.

If the appointment is for a conference or meeting on your premises s/he may find it useful to know what time it is likely to end and what catering facilities are available.

16 *Always* write clearly!

Activity 7.1.1

You know you should *never* double-book, but whilst you were on holiday a stand-in for you has double-booked your employer in the diary. You have only just discovered the mistake and the appointment is for tomorrow. What would you do?

Diary management

Good diary management is a technique which can be learnt and developed. Well-organised, well-planned diaries will enable busy executives and their assistants to make the very best use of time available. Your work diary is likely to be more full than your employer's as yours will have more detail of the tasks to be carried out.

Your employer's diary

MONDAY 15 AUGUST 1992

0900

0930

1000

1030 Meeting with Mr. King e Associates. Finance Office

1100

1130

1200

1230 Lunch at Grand Hotel with Mr. Simmons Sales Director Karins PLC. 021-224 4073

Your own diary

MONDAY 5 AUGUST 1992

0900 Order Coffee e biscuits - E's room for 10.30a.m

0930 Papers for next month's Sales meeting to be sent out.

1000 Check files for finance meeting - to E.

1030

1100 Check availability of room for interviews 24/8

1130 Arrange taxi for E for 12.15p.m. (286 1249)

1200 Insurance report to be collected e edited

1230 E. lunching with Mr. Simmons Sales director Karins PLC at Grand Hotel 081-229 4073

Activity 7.1.2

You are an administrative assistant working for a firm of accountants. Your boss is Tim Cross who is one of the partners in the firm. He also has special responsibilities for health and safety in the firm. The following entries need to be made in the diaries of both yourself and Mr Cross for the morning of Tuesday 3 September 199-.

1 At 9.00 am the new junior clerk is to be introduced to staff and given a short initial induction into the firm.

2 There is a meeting at 12.30 pm of the local Chartered Accountants' Association at the Red Lion Hotel, Islington. Telephone number of the secretary is 071-447 2301. The meeting includes lunch but is only likely to last 1½–2 hours.

3 Mrs Jenner of 32 Bristol Lane, Willesden (Tel: 081-653 2198) is coming to see Mr Cross at 11.00 am to discuss her financial situation.

4 Mr Cross is visiting Porter & Porter re their VAT situation on his way into work. They are at 67-89 New Street, Stoke Newington (Tel: 071-249 2133).

5 Minutes of the last health and safety committee meeting to be typed. They need to be sent out today.

6 At 10.30 am a half-hour demonstration is to be given on a new item of accounting software. Mr Cross specifically wishes you to see it.

7 Mr Cross has said he would like to have a word with the new junior at a convenient time.

Mr Cross's diary

TUESDAY 3 SEPTEMBER 199-

0900
0930
1000
1030
1100
1130
1200
1230
1300

Your own diary

TUESDAY 3 SEPTEMBER 199-
0900
0930
1000
1030
1100
1130
1200
1230
1300

How would you ensure that both diaries were kept up-to-date, legible and accurate?

Several businesses now have networked computerised diary facilities. This enables the person wishing to call a meeting at a specific time to check the 'screen' diaries of staff to find out whether or not they have prior engagements.

In addition, the electronic organiser will allow the user to check the calendar to see whether there are any appointments on a specific date. A week's or month's engagements may be scanned and hard copy of sections obtained as required.

Activity 7.1.3

Your present employer has a traditional diary but s/he is interested in knowing more about electronic systems. S/he has asked you to find out as much information as you can about such diaries and to set out your findings on a fact sheet.

Appointment scheduling aids

There are various aids to help organise appointments. In addition to a diary, a wall planner or visual chart is useful for recording appointments as well as meetings, holidays, conferences and target dates. Coloured and labelled signalling devices may be used with these aids to prompt the user.

A follow-up system or bring-forward system are aids to ensure that our memory is jogged and that we perform certain tasks on a particular day. These also ensure that we are fully aware that appointments have been made for a certain time.

HOLIDAY ROTA 199-													
	MAY		JUNE				JULY					AUGUST	
	21	28	4	11	18	25	2	9	16	23	30	6	13
J. Thomas			O	O							O		
R. Smith					O				O	O			
D. Watson	O	O	O										
L. Evans							O	O				O	
F. Smart								O				O	O

Wall planner

Follow-up systems

An example of such a system is where sections or pockets in a filing cabinet, card index or concertina file are set aside, one for each day of the month and one for each month of the year.

When an appointment is made the details are recorded on a card. This is then placed in the system in the appropriate day or month pocket for when the appointment is to take place.

At the beginning of each month the user would place the various cards from the current month into the appropriate day pockets.

Each day the user would check the system to see what tasks need to be done.

Activity 7.1.4

Create a simple bring-forward or follow-up system for yourself using the most appropriate, available equipment.

Prepare cards for items which need a 'follow-up' and place these in your system as appropriate. Regularly check the system. How well is it working?

You may wish to add personal appointments in addition to those connected with your employment.

Element 7.2 – Organise own work schedule

Do you have a set routine for the day? If 'yes' have you worked out this routine or has someone else dictated it for you? Do you do the jobs you like first and leave difficult tasks to the end of the day? What determines the priority you give to a particular task – the status of the person handing out the task or some other factor?

How organised are you – do you have good desk-top management?

Are you in control?

How do you decide which jobs should be completed first? It is necessary to plan work in order to ensure that tasks are completed on time. These tasks may be:

1 **Routine tasks** which usually have to be completed within set periods, for example, invoices and statements dated for one day need to be posted or standard letters may be sent out on a regular basis – weekly, monthly, yearly. These are the easiest tasks to cope with. They are 'expected' and are slotted into the everyday procedures of the business.

2 **Expected heavy workload** which may be anticipated. You may know when you will be extra busy, for example, the end of the financial month is invariably a very busy time for anyone connected with an accounts department or during the summer months when staff are on holiday. It should be possible to programme such work in advance, maybe in preference to less important work.

3 **Unexpected heavy workload** which may affect your schedule at any time, for example, changing to a computerised filing system or an exhibition or promotion. If well planned, extra work may be incorporated in the normal daily workload.

4 **Emergencies** which cannot be programmed in advance, for example, computer or photocopier breakdown. It is necessary to reschedule tasks immediately and/or make alternative arrangements if equipment breakdown is involved.

Activity 7.2.1

List all the tasks you carried out on your last, full working day and try to categorise them into the four situations above. Did you have a busy day? If so did it run smoothly because you were in control or was it chaotic.

Prioritising tasks to be carried out

How can we decide which are our priorities and which tasks can safely be left until later or delegated to a subordinate (see also Unit 6).

Spend a few moments writing down clearly all tasks to be completed. Referring to the questions below put them into an order of priority.

1 What are the likely effects of completing or not completing the task on:

   a) the company's image/good relations with its customers and members of staff;

   b) on other people;

   c) on other people's jobs.

2 If you work for several people – Who is the work for? Whose work takes priority?

3 How much time is required to carry out the task satisfactorily? Is the time required available? If not are you able to ask for other people's help and/or are you able to delegate the work so that it is completed satisfactorily?

4 When is the deadline for this particular task?

5 Do you require any specific resources, for example, a word processor or seminar room, and are they available or not?

6 Do you need to consult/liaise with another member of staff and are they available or not?

It is necessary to keep this plan flexible to accommodate any emergencies which may arise. It is also good practice to train and develop less experienced members of staff and encourage them to carry out some of the tasks.

It is useful to have pre-prepared photocopied sheets for your action programme. An example of the type of aid you would find useful is shown below.

Date _____

	Tasks – in priority order	Action completed	Further action required	Given to
1				
2				
3				
4				
5				

Action programme

Activity 7.2.2

You are an administrative assistant working in the personnel department of a large company. Below is a list of tasks needed to be carried out by you this afternoon before you go off on two weeks' holiday.

1 Reply to a letter from a school leaver asking your advice on career prospects with the company.

2 Read three company circulars. You are top of the circulation list and these documents have been on your desk for two weeks.

3 Attend a monthly safety meeting 2.00-3.00pm.

4 You have a list of ten people in the company to phone about their reply to a questionnaire that was distributed to all staff. Their response needs to be known by next Tuesday.

5 A request from wages and salaries for you to update your personal details. To be returned by next Friday.

6 Final arrangements for a computer awareness course for new recruits needs to be completed. At least an hour's work is required. It is due to commence the Monday you return from your holidays.

Set out these tasks in order of priority, giving an approximate time for their completion and an explanation as to why you have chosen the order. Are there any tasks which you would delegate?

Time management

If you are always short of time, one way of improving the organisation of your own work schedule is to consider carefully *how* you actually work. Tick 'Yes'/'No' box as appropriate.

Yes/No

- Do you believe that *every* piece of work has to be 100% perfect?

- Do you read every word of every communication sent to you?

- Do you agree with the statement 'If you want a job done well you must do it yourself'?

- Do you normally work through your lunch break?

- Do you frequently give up your social life because of pressures of work?

- Do you resent the time spent discussing a problem with colleagues when you could have made the decision yourself in a few minutes?

If you have ticked 'Yes' in three or more of the boxes it would suggest that either you have spare time or that you are not looking at your priorities carefully enough.

If you answered 'Yes' to all of the above it would suggest that you are not using your time effectively. Maybe you need to delegate and train junior staff to take on some of your workload.

Stress management

It is generally accepted that relaxed, happy workers lead to higher productivity. Stress can cause a once capable worker to be ineffective and unproductive. Always be aware of the areas where stress may occur.

Stress may arise from physical or mental situations. Being placed in an out-of-the-way office with little contact with main office staff can make an individual anxious and stressed. Likewise, a situation where you are working as an assistant to more than one executive, all wanting your immediate attention, can lead to conflict and an unhappy and stressful working environment. In contrast, having too little work to do may also cause stress!

Learn to recognise stress, try to combat its effects and save time by:

At work

1 Looking at your work routine very carefully. Prioritise tasks each day and leave less urgent ones for another time.

2 Spending time at the start of each task to ensure that you fully understand the task in hand and so avoid any effort being wasted.

3 Always writing down important information given to you. Carry a notebook around with you if necessary. Even if you have a good memory it is impossible to expect to remember every detail of every discussion you have.

4 Following good desk-top management practice. An untidy desk is a prime location for losing important documents.

5 Following all recognised efficiency procedures for filing – whether computerised or traditional. It may save you many frustrating hours looking for a file or document and reduce your stress level enormously.

6 Using visual planning and control aids whenever appropriate.

7 Being more assertive.

8 Being positive. Knowing and valuing your own talents.

9 Recognising stress reaction in others.

At home

10 Learning to relax, sitting with your feet up or taking a hot bath.

11 Listening to soothing music (there are special tapes available).

12 Reading books or magazines that are not related to your work.

13 Starting a new hobby or rediscovering an old one.

14 Taking up sport or joining a health club.

15 Going away on holiday even if it is just to visit family or friends.

UNIT
7

Work-related task

TASK ONE – Elements 7.1 and 7.2

There are five sections in the private sports centre where you work:

1 Centre manager's section headed by John Fenwick.

2 Marketing and promotions section headed by Susan Painter.

3 Personnel and recruitment section headed by Jack Metcalfe.

4 Purchasing section headed by Harry Chan.

5 Administration office which you have recently joined as office manager. Your staff consists of two clerk/typists, one of whom is a temp, and a junior.

Your company is in business to provide a range of sporting facilities to the general public and business organisations. There is a private members' social club attached to the centre as well as a sportswear retail outlet. Meetings for members are held regularly and it is the job of the administration staff to prepare the necessary details and, in addition, to provide full office/secretarial services to the centre.

You are also responsible for looking after the diaries and appointments of Mr Fenwick, the centre manager, and Ms Painter, the marketing and promotions manager.

It is Monday 23 September 1992 and their appointments for the day are as shown below:

Extract from John Fenwick's diary

MONDAY 23 SEPTEMBER 199-

10.00 am Appt. Mr Pearson - 'Carters' 061-224489

Extract from Susan Painter's diary

MONDAY 23 SEPTEMBER 199-

10.30 am Appt. Mr. David Fox 'Duckworths' 081-259 7789

Extract from your own diary

MONDAY 23 SEPTEMBER 199-

9.00 am   Holiday dates to J. Metcalfe

10.00 am   JF Appt. Mr. Pearson (Carters Ctl- 224489)

10.30 am   SP Appt. Mr. David Fox (Duckworths
           081- 259.7789)

          Contact Employment Agency for Temp.

You have to organise the following jobs for the administration staff:

1. 150 circular letters must be inserted into envelopes, franked and sent off by the mid-day post. These are to be sent to all 16 to18-year-old club members.

2. A circular letter inviting 400 potential customers to attend a promotions buffet lunch to be held in four weeks' time.

3. Typing – there are nine items marked 'urgent' stacked in a 'work today' tray. Behind the folders are a further ten folders marked 'non-urgent'.

4. There are six unopened boxes of stationery which have just been delivered and they are downstairs in reception. It appears that two of the boxes contain letterheaded paper.

5. There is a telephone message from BAY Computers who are sending one of their representatives to the centre this morning to give a demonstration on a new computer communications link.

6. There is a message on your desk from an employment agency. They are offering another temp to start next week.

7. Jack Metcalfe wants the holiday dates of your staff today.

8. There are two bulky folders of invoices which need to be sorted out and checked against copy order forms.

9. There are four large lever arch files on purchases which require work. All the contents need to be sorted out in order. There are other documents in your in-tray which need to be photocopied and inserted into the four lever arch files. Harry Chan requires them urgently.

10. There is an audio-tape on your desk from Ms Painter with a memo that she wants it within the next hour. After listening to the tape, you realise it is going to take more than an hour to type the work.

11. Forty envelopes have been sealed and you discover there are still a number of important documents which need to go into the envelopes.

12. Your best clerk/typist is going on holiday next week. You need to contact an employment agency for a temp.

13 A note from the social membership secretary that two of the centre members' committees are to be held in two weeks' time. Agendas are enclosed. The notice and agenda for the meetings needs to be typed and sent out to committee members. The details are to be placed on the wall planner.

14 A note of complaint from Susan Painter about the office junior's rudeness when she asked her to make the tea for her and a client on Friday afternoon.

During the morning

1 Mr Pearson has phoned in to ask whether his appointment booked for 10.00 am with Mr Fenwick could be put back to 10.30 am.

2 A member of the centre staff comes to you and asked to speak very urgently with Mr Fenwick this morning about a personal matter.

3 At 10.00 am a highly respected and influential customer has arrived wanting to see Ms Painter about a conference he would like to hold at the centre.

Also

1 You have run out of letterheaded paper in the office.

2 The disc containing the contents of the circular letter for the promotions buffet lunch is missing.

3 A cheque for £5000 has gone missing.

How would you deal with this situation? Make out an action programme and indicate which tasks you would carry out yourself, which you would delegate and which leave till later. Show the entries you would make in the diaries.

What are your comments about the backlog of work and the items which have gone missing?

Servicing meetings

Main elements covered
8.1   Organise and prepare for meetings
8.2   Administer and take notes of meetings

Supplementary elements covered
2.2   Locate and abstract information from unspecified sources
2.3   Organise and present information in a variety of formats
5.1   Produce text from oral and written material using an alphanumeric
      keyboard

Element 8.1 – Organise and prepare for meetings

In your role as an administrative assistant you may often be called on to organise meetings, to undertake the administrative work associated with them and sometimes to attend them.

Meetings are called so that a group of people may discuss a variety of topics with all those present having the opportunity to give their views.

Meetings may be held by committees, associations and other organisations. They may be very formal, for example, the Annual General Meeting (AGM) of a Public Limited Company (PLC) or less formal, for example, a weekly meeting of section heads to discuss mutual problems. The documentation and procedures followed will therefore vary from meeting to meeting.

Committee meetings

A committee is a group of individuals drawn from a much wider group and given terms of reference to carry out a particular function. Committees will often hold regular meetings. Such meetings are attended by those selected to serve on the Committee.

**FACT
FINDER**

There are various types of committee:

- **Ad hoc committee.** This committee is formed for a specific purpose such as to arrange a fund raising event. Once the work has been completed the committee is disbanded.

- **Advisory committee.** As its name suggests this is a group of individuals with a specific expertise who meet and discuss matters of policy relevant to their particular terms of reference and make recommendations to other organisations if appropriate.

- **Executive committee.** Members may be elected or chosen to sit on this committee which has wide-ranging powers to manage an organisation and formulate its policy.

- **Standing committee.** This is a committee which is permanently established to deal with on-going matters, such as health and safety.

- **Statutory committee.** Some committees are referred to as statutory because there is a legal obligation for them to be formed, for example, local government education and housing committees.

- **Sub-committee.** This is a group of individuals nominated by the parent committee and given particular matters to investigate. The sub-committee must keep within its terms of reference and it would need to report back regularly to the main committee.

The annual general meeting of a company

131

Activity 8.1.1

Find out the types of meetings and committees which operate either where you work or where you study. List them and give the functions of the committees, and if possible state how frequently they meet.

Main points to consider when arranging a meeting

1 *When* is the meeting to be held? The date of a meeting should be fixed well in advance so that the people involved should be free to attend.

2 *Where* is the meeting to be held? The location needs to be appropriate for the number of people likely to attend.

3 *Who* is to be invited? Make sure you have a full list of those who are entitled to attend.

4 *How* will the meeting be called? By a formal notice sent out to those entitled to attend, a memo, a telephone call, a press notice, details placed on a notice board or will it be just a verbal communication?

   Some meetings may be able to be called and arranged via a company's management information system, through the electronic diary facility.

5 *Why* is the meeting being called? What items will be on the agenda?

Activity 8.1.2

Investigate the different basis on which people can attend a meeting. In this context, what is meant by the terms:

Ex officio; In attendance; Elected member; Co-opted member?

Set out your findings on a fact sheet.

Documentation

For formal meetings a written **notice** is usually sent out to those entitled to attend. It should state the type of meeting, for example, an AGM, and the date, time and the place where the meeting will be held. It should also give the name and designation of the convenor and the date on which the notice is sent out. When notification of the annual general meeting is sent to shareholders of a company, a **form of proxy** will accompany the notice together with a copy of the **annual report and accounts** of the company.

Normally 21 clear days' notice is given before an annual general meeting and seven to 14 clear days' notice for other meetings.

Activity 8.1.3

Find out what is meant by a proxy vote and who is entitled to have one. Try to obtain an original or a photocopy of a form of proxy for a company.

The **agenda** is a list of items to be discussed at the meeting. These are standard items, in a set order, which usually appear on an agenda alongside new items for discussion, as follows:

AGENDA

1 Apologies for absence

2 Minutes of the previous meeting

3 Matters arising from the minutes

4 New agenda items

5 Any other business (often abbreviated to AOB)

6 Date, time and venue of next meeting.

With less formal meetings it is normal practice to include the agenda with the notice, see the example below.

Example of agenda with notice

BARNWOOD PLC SALES PROMOTION TEAM COMMITTEE

A meeting of the Sales Promotion Team will be held in Committee Room 4 on Wednesday 12 June 199- at 2.00 pm.

AGENDA

1   Apologies for absence

2   Minutes of the last meeting

3   Matters arising from the minutes

4   Finances - report from Chairperson

5   New contacts

6   Tele-sales project

7   Any other business

8   Date of next meeting

R Bains
Secretary

22 May 199-

Activity 8.1.4

Prepare a notice and agenda for the next meeting of the sales promotion committee to be held on Wednesday 10 July at the same time and place. In addition to the latest situation with finances the committee is to discuss a sponsorship presentation.

Common terms

There are many terms used in connection with meetings. As an administrative assistant involved with meetings it is useful to have a clear understanding of some of the more commonly used ones.

**FACT
FINDER**

Terms connected with meetings procedure include:

Quorum

This is the minimum number of members who must be present for the meeting to begin. Should members leave the meeting and the quorum is lost, the meeting should be adjourned, otherwise the decisions subsequently taken at that meeting will be invalid.

Adjournment

A meeting may be adjourned *after* it has commenced, for example, because the time allowed has run out or there is no quorum. The meeting will then recommence at a later date.

Postponement

A meeting may be postponed even *before* it has commenced maybe because there is no quorum. The meeting may then be rescheduled for a future date.

Motion

A motion is a proposal which may have been handed in before the meeting so that it can be an item on the agenda. It requires a proposer and seconder before it can be discussed by the members.

Resolution

A resolution is a formal decision passed at a meeting.

Simple majority

When taking a vote, only one extra vote in favour is required for the proposal to be accepted.

Two-thirds majority

When voting, at least two-thirds of those present vote in favour for the proposal to be accepted.

Proxy vote

This allows for those unable to attend a meeting to nominate a person to vote on their behalf. Special forms for such arrangements are usually prepared.

Activity 8.1.5

1 There are other terms connected with the procedure at meetings than the ones already mentioned. Research the following terms and place written explanations of them on your file:

Rider; Lie on the table; Point of order; Right of reply.

2 Research and write up the differences between the following terms:

a) A vote has been passed 'unanimously' or *nem con*.
b) Someone who is 'present' and someone who is 'in attendance'.
c) A 'casting vote' and a 'proxy vote'.

Accommodation

It is important to book appropriate accommodation well in advance of the date of the meeting. If those attending are travelling some distance it may be an advantage for the venue to be relatively close to a railway station. If it is an international meeting then proximity to an airport may be a consideration.

Check that your venue is able to provide the special facilities you need. Some members attending the meeting may have special dietary requirements or some may be in wheelchairs and require ease of access. Translation facilities may be required if there are overseas members. Medical facilities may also be needed.

You should check whether the venue follows good safety practices and how easy it would be to evacuate the building in the case of an emergency.

Activity 8.1.6

A rebuilding programme has started at your company headquarters so all board meetings will have to be held off-site during the next six months. Your employer has asked you to investigate three local hotels or centres offering meeting venues. Find out whether they are able to provide special facilities, such as those mentioned above. What prices do they charge?

Set out your findings in a memo to your employer, Mr David Khan.

Meetings can be extremely frustrating for those attending if they are not properly controlled. It is the chairperson's duty to ensure that everyone entitled to be present has the opportunity to speak.

FACT FINDER

Chairperson's duties

1 Approve the agenda which will probably have been prepared by the meetings secretary.

2 Ensure that a quorum of entitled members is present at all times throughout the meeting.

3 Sign the minutes of the previous meeting when they have been approved by members of the meeting.

4 Ensure the agenda is followed unless the meeting agrees otherwise.

5 Encourage everyone to participate and control those who seem to want to monopolise the meeting.

6 Summarise discussions when appropriate.

7 End the meeting positively.

It is useful to state how long the meeting will last at the beginning of discussions. If members know there is a time limit they will not be tempted to wander from the point under discussion. A 'timed' agenda may help.

It is also good practice to have a limited number of items for discussion. A very long meeting can lead to boredom and poor decisions.

Activity 8.1.7

A chairperson may use a different style of agenda to the one given to other members present at the meeting. How is it different? Find an example of such an agenda and place it on your file.

Rules

How do we know the rules that a particular organisation should follow? The rules applicable to meetings are included in the **articles of association** of a company, **standing orders** of local government committees and the **rules** or **constitution** of other bodies.

FACT FINDER

Rules to be followed at meetings for a particular organisation may specify:

1 Powers, functions and responsibilities of the meeting.

2 Persons entitled to attend the meeting.

3 Eligibility of those wishing to stand for office, the procedure for their election and the duration of their service.

4 The frequency of meetings.

5 The numbers of members required to be present to form a quorum.

6 The powers of the meeting to co-opt new members.

7 The ex officio privileges of officers.

8 Voting rights and voting procedures.

Activity 8.1.8

As chairperson of a meeting what would you do in the following circumstances?

1 There has been a lengthy discussion on a topic and members are becoming restless.

2 Twenty members are a quorum, there are now only 18 members present. You are expecting another three members to arrive later.

3 Some information on an item under discussion is not available.

4 There is an urgent telephone call and you must leave immediately

Duties to be carried out before the meeting

As an administrative assistant you may be solely responsible for organising all arrangements for meetings and/or acting as secretary to the meeting.

Always make sure that you have a written check-list of the work to be done. Tick off items as the work is completed.

**FACT
FINDER**

Check-list of work to be done before the meeting

1 Confirm time and date with your supervisor and check if there are any special requirements, for example, translation equipment.

2 Check that details of the meeting are in any diaries for which you are responsible.

3 Book an appropriate venue. Check that the meeting room is accessible for disabled persons, if necessary. Confirm in writing as appropriate.

4 Open a file for any papers or notes which relate to the meeting.

5 Check whether there are any specific papers for members to read before the meeting. If so, obtain copies, as appropriate.

6 Circulate the agenda for the meeting together with confirmation of the time and date and any papers members need to read.

7 Collect spare copies of all paper work, so that this is available at the meeting.

8 Prepare place names if appropriate. It may be necessary at this stage to prepare a seating plan for the meeting. If this is necessary you should take into consideration the type of meeting – whether it is formal or informal. With formal meetings it is customary for officers and the chairman, in particular, to be in a focal position.

9 Arrange audio-visual aids and equipment if necessary, for example, an overhead projector or flip chart.

10 If appropriate, arrange for refreshments to be served and/or water/soft drinks to be on the table.

11 Ensure there are plenty of pens and paper in stock should they be required.

Activity 8.1.9

Your employer acts as secretary to monthly internal management committee meetings. One of her/his tasks is to prepare the notice of the meeting and agenda, and distribute them to the management team at least one week before the date of the meeting. In practice, this job is delegated to you as her/his assistant. How would you:

1 Obtain items for the agenda?

2 Decide which items should be included in the agenda?

3 Make sure that you kept to your schedule and had all the completed documents distributed in time?

Element 8.2 – Administer and take notes of meetings

Even with the best organisation and well laid plans things can go wrong. **Always check on the day to be sure your arrangements are as they should be.**

FACT FINDER

Check-list of work to be done on the day of the meeting

1 Check that the room is ready, has sufficient chairs and that the ventilation and heating are satisfactory. Place a notice on the door that a 'meeting is in progress'.

2 In order that those attending the meeting do not lose their way, place notices where appropriate and if necessary give details of the meeting to reception and the security staff.

3 Ensure spare copies of all documents are at hand.

4 If name cards are used, set them out appropriately on the conference table or leave them by the entrance if members are choosing their own seats. It is sometimes useful to have an overall plan of the seating arrangements.

It is customary for the chairperson to sit at the head of the table and, if appropriate, the secretary on his/her right-hand side and the treasurer on the left.

Chairperson

Secretary   Treasurer

5 Ensure that water and glasses are available, plus ashtrays, if smoking is allowed by members.

6 Prepare an attendance sheet if required.

7 If you are to take notes or minutes of the meeting make sure you know what the meeting is about and try to familiarise yourself with the names of those likely to be present.

8 Ensure the minute book is available for the chairperson's signature.

9 It is sensible to be prepared for any sudden illness which may be suffered by any members attending the meeting. There may be a doctor attached to the hotel where the meeting is being held or you may have a company nurse. Make sure you know where the nearest telephone is located and the telephone number to call medical help quickly.

Activity 8.2.1

As an administrative assistant to your employer who is chairperson for the meeting you have various problems to deal with.

1 One member arrives early with a lighted cigarette although it is the clear policy of the committee that their meetings should be non-smoking.

2 An individual arrives who you do not know and who is not on your list of members. You do not have copies of the documents for her.

How would you deal with these situations?

Procedures during the meeting

If you are in charge of arrangements during the meeting it is necessary to ensure that certain actions are carried out. Without following laid-down procedures the meeting may be invalid.

Ensure everyone signs the attendance sheet or that you take a note of those present. Such information may be important in the future to confirm that a member has been present. Also ensure that the chairperson checks that a quorum is present at all times.

Activity 8.2.2

Which of the following do you consider to be the duty of the chairperson and which the duty of the secretary of the meeting?

1 Approve the agenda.

2 Send out the notice of meeting.

3 Control the behaviour of members at a meeting.

4 Take the minutes.

5 Give permission to speak.

6 Ensure that a quorum is present at all times.

7 Sign minutes.

8 Record the exact wording of resolutions.

9 Take charge of the attendance sheet.

10 End the meeting.

FACT FINDER

Check-list of work to be done after the meeting

1 Place a copy of the signed minutes into the minute book.

2 Clear up the meeting room unless it is someone else's job. Ensure all spare copies of documents are disposed of carefully and other documents returned to files.

3 As soon as possible draft notes or minutes of the meeting including an action column as appropriate.

4 Obtain the chairperson's approval of draft minutes/notes.

5 When the draft minutes have been approved, distribute them.

6 Check that the date of the next meeting is in your own and your employer's diary.

7 Deal with any matters arising from the meeting – ensure all 'action' is carried out.

8 Make a note of special points for the agenda of the next meeting.

Activity 8.2.3

Many of the documents used at meetings are of a sensitive nature. Some are highly confidential.

You are the minutes secretary at board meetings of a drug company. You have been warned by your employer that there are people who would not hesitate to steal or obtain by false means the information on decisions taken at these meetings. What would you do to ensure that the correct security and confidentiality measures are followed at all times?

A written record of meetings

It is very important that what has occurred at a meeting is recorded. This may take the form of minutes, a report, a summary or notes. Whichever form is used it should be an accurate and clear recording of what was decided.

**FACT
FINDER**

Some hints for taking an accurate and clear record of proceedings at a meeting

1 Before the meeting read through the record of a previous meeting.

2 Before the meeting make sure you know what the meeting is going to be about. Then have a look at the agenda and familiarise yourself with the items to be discussed.

3 Refer to the list of those attending the meeting and attempt to identify them. It is helpful to draw a chart before the meeting showing the position of each person present and her/his name.

4 Sit where you can hear clearly, listen carefully to what is being said and take brief notes on each item on the agenda. (It may be necessary to sit near the door if you need to call in someone who is to attend the meeting for one item only.)

Always write concisely, simply and clearly, remembering at all times that accuracy is vital.

Avoid long and involved sentences – they may be ambiguous or confusing. If you do not hear or understand anything say so.

Only take down the main points discussed and agreements reached. However, take care to record **verbatim** (word for word) any motions, resolutions and amendments as appropriate, together with names of proposers and seconders.

Where the number of votes have been counted these should be shown. Also it is usually noted whether a motion has been carried 'unanimously' or *nem con* (the vote has been carried with no one voting against but some members have abstained). Always check the style used by your particular organisation.

(A good chairperson will summarise discussions – this should be invaluable to you.)

5   Write down who will be responsible for any action to be carried out before the next meeting. Some organisations put names or initials of those to carry out specific tasks in an action column on the right-hand side of the record.

6   Write up draft notes or minutes as soon as possible after the meeting while the discussion is still fresh in your mind. Do not throw your original notes away until the draft notes or minutes of the meeting have been approved.

Minutes of a meeting

A minute is a record of what was *decided* at a meeting. There are different styles of minute.

A full minute would consist of five elements:

1   The **number** of the minute.

2   The **subject** of the minute.

3   A short paragraph **summarising** the discussion.

4   The **outcome** – the resolution or agreement reached.

5   The **action** column – if appropriate.

Example of a minute

```
102/92    PURCHASE OF COMPUTERS

          A report was presented to the meeting
          on the various computers which had been
          on the recommendation list for purchase.

          It was agreed that three ROK computers would be
          purchased at a total cost of £16 500. Mr Baker
          to prepare the order.                        RB
```

Points to note
1   Reported speech must be used.

2   The names of those who have spoken at the meeting are not normally recorded.

3   The style is impersonal. Your own personal views should not be recorded!

4   In minutes of formal meetings words such as AGREED and RESOLVED are sometimes typed out in capitals to emphasise decisions that have been taken.

Activity 8.2.4

Prepare a minute from the following text.

Hon Secretary: There is someone who has been put forward for election –

143

Jane Prince. She has been proposed by the treasurer and seconded by the chair.

Chair: Those in favour of Miss Prince's election? Those against? I declare Miss Prince unanimously elected a member of the Barnwood Sports Club. Will our membership secretary please ensure she is given all details of the club.

The following is an example of the minutes of a meeting. You should appreciate this is not necessarily *the* style – companies and committees will have their own style and you should follow their guidelines.

Example of a set of minutes

MINUTES OF THE BARNWOOD PLC SALES PROMOTION TEAM MONTHLY MEETING HELD IN COMMITTEE ROOM 4 ON WEDNESDAY 12 JUNE 199- AT 2.00 PM

```
Present:      M McLean (Chairperson)
              R Bains
              J Britton
              L Cooper
              R Patel (Secretary)
```

1	APOLOGIES	L Carter
2	MINUTES	The minutes of the meeting held on Wednesday 15 May 199- were approved and signed by the Chairperson.
3	MATTERS ARISING	There were no matters arising.
4	FINANCES	It was stated that the budget was causing some concern. The company had overspent during the first quarter of the year and would need to make up the shortfall by the end of July.
5	PROMOTION TEAM'S NEW PROJECTS	Letters had been received from four further organisations agreeing to allow the promotion team on their premises. If the plan goes well it should mean many new outlets for the company's products. L Cooper agreed to send details of these contacts to team members. LC

```
6   TELE-SALES        It was stated that the tele-sales
                      project was running well although
                      training had been held up due to
                      sickness. R Bains agreed to send
                      everyone a copy of the new training
                      programme.                      RB

7   ANY OTHER         There was none.
    BUSINESS

8   DATE OF NEXT      The date of the next meeting was
    MEETING           provisionally fixed for Wednesday
                      10 July at 2.00 pm in Committee
                      Room 4. R Patel to check the
                      booking of the room.            RP


Signed ................... Chairperson

Date .....................
```

Work-related tasks

UNIT 8

You (Jack) are working as administrative assistant to Mr Gregson who is managing director of Cusack & Cusack PLC.

It is Tuesday and you have been out of the office all day at a meeting and you know Mr Gregson will be away on a conference tomorrow and Thursday. Unfortunately you have been held up in the traffic. You find the following messages waiting for you on your answering machine together with some papers when you eventually get to the office.

TASK 1 – Element 8.1

```
Jack This is Jim Gregson here. Sorry I missed you.

I forgot to mention I shall be holding an Executive
Committee Meeting three weeks tomorrow. I think we need
to send out the notice within the next couple of days. I
would like to use the main board room as there will be
quite a few of us and we have some of our continental
sales people coming over. I want to start at 2 o'clock
sharp - there are a few important things to discuss and
I expect all senior executives to attend. They must let
me know beforehand if there is any reason why they won't
be able to come. Will you draft out the Agenda - here's
a list of items I'll be dealing with.

• Progress report on new customer credit scheme.
```

- Insurance company's report on fire damage at the Southern Branch offices.

- Proposed take-over of the Golden Garden Hotel.

- Annual budget for computing hardware.

- Appointment of new Chief Accountant.

Please send this out with a memo to everyone who is on the list (attached) telling them the time, date, etc. Would you also send copies of the documents out to Spain and Italy. We haven't got much time so send them the quickest way possible.

Make sure to book the main board room and leave me a note that this is OK.

As this is a special meeting would you also arrange for Mrs Harris to put on some really nice refreshments for our guests.

Thanks

You decide to let your Junior help you with this work. After drafting the agenda you give it to her/him to type up for you.

You also ask her/him to prepare an envelope for each of the members on the Executive Committee in the UK and prepare a fax for those at the Spanish and Italian offices.

LIST OF STAFF ON EXECUTIVE COMMITTEE

Jo Johnson - Company Secretary

Ann McKenna - Personnel Manager

James Kent - Financial Manager

Peter Khan - Marketing Manager

Michael Allen - Project Manager

Rachel Stephenson - Office Manager

Spanish Office: Carlos Tavio, 2341 Via Real, Madrid

Italian Office: Giorgio Sclisizzi, 32876 Via Garibaldi, Rome

TASK TWO – Element 8.2

Second message

Jack

By the way I've left the agenda of the meeting I went to today on your desk. As the Secretary was off sick I said I would prepare the minutes. I've scribbled some notes on it. Hope you can make sense of it. If you put it on the word processor I can amend it when I get back on Friday.

Below is the agenda document that has been left on your desk:

EUROPEAN BUSINESS CONTACTS ASSOCIATION

A meeting of the European Business Contacts Association will be held at Leon House, Westgate, London W1 at 2.00 pm on Tuesday 25 June 199-

A G E N D A

1   Apologies for absence *Paulo Musoni, Ron Robertson*

2   Minutes of Meeting held Tuesday 21 May 199- *Fine*

3   Matters arising from minutes *None*

4   Correspondence *① letter from Ann King - thanks for card e flowers whilst in hospital*
② Enquiry from Julio Martos wishing to become member. Invite to next meeting

5   Proposed visit to Milan *⑤ Arrangements in hand Cost would be £378·00 for 4 days. Partners invited. Need to know Numbers by 31-7-9- at latest.*

6   October Business Exhibition

7   Any other business *⑥ Piete André in charge Members to prepare their own items for display - should liase with P e A.*

8   Date of next meeting *3rd Tuesday in July - same time e place*

Mark McDonald

Secretary

12069-

Present
Jack Raiver (chair)
Me (deputising Ron Robertson)
Jill Cranshaw (Treasurer)
+ Kurt Svendsen, Piet Lenain, André Van Doren, Sabine Place e Barbara Graf.

To further develop your competence for this unit you may need to carry out various role-playing situations in addition to obtaining as much practical experience as possible in the work place.

Role-playing situation suggestions

With your fellow students/work colleagues form a committee to:

1 Arrange a company outing.

2 Organise a fund-raising event.

3 Organise a presentation to retiring members of your company.

4 Arrange a friendly sports competition with a neighbouring company or college.

Notes:
Individuals should take it in turn to role play the various parts, i.e. chairperson, secretary, and book and prepare the room for the meeting, sending out a notice and agenda for each meeting.

Participants should write up the meeting in note or minute form.

Office resource administration

Main elements covered
9.1   Maintain office supplies
9.2   Maintain a petty cash system
9.3   Ensure the use of authorised banking procedures

Supplementary elements covered
2.3   Organise and present information in a variety of formats
5.1   Produce text from oral and written material using an alphanumeric
      keyboard

Element 9.1 – Maintain office supplies

The main aims of stock control procedures are to:

**1 Account for all purchases of goods and materials and to ensure the
prompt despatch of processed or manufactured goods to customers.**

Without a quick response to customers' requests for goods, valuable orders
could easily be lost.

2 Avoid any wastage or loss of goods.

Some items in stock may be perishable and may only keep for a short time.
Expensive goods may require special facilities to prevent pilfering. Also there
may be considerable wastage if new stock is used instead of old.

3 Ensure that stock is conveniently located.

The most commonly used items should be easily accessible with heavy items
near floor level to avoid risk of injury. Due care should be given to the effect
on stock of damp and fire and the risk of breakage to fragile items.

4 Decide on appropriate stock levels.

A maximum and minimum level of stock needs to be decided for each item.
Such levels should take into account the rate of use and restocking time
required. The controller must always ensure that stock is available otherwise
administration may grind to a halt if stationery runs out. This in turn may
affect the profitability of the organisation.

5 Supervise the control of stores and the issue of stock.

Activity 9.1.1

Items such as bond and bank paper, printer ribbons, pencils, staples and paper clips are just a few examples of what may be categorised as **office supplies**. Prepare a list of all such items setting out your data on an information sheet giving as much detail as possible.

To ensure that office supplies are satisfactorily maintained we require a control system that consists of proper procedures for: a) the requisitioning and ordering of supplies; b) the recording of the receipt of those supplies; c) the allocation and recording of supplies to staff; and d) allowing for regular stock-taking.

Systems for controlling stock range from simple recording and calculation to sophisticated computerised systems.

FACT

FINDER

Depending on the item being stored there are several methods for controlling stock.

A visual system

One example of a visual system is where coloured tabs or similar are inserted, at the reorder level, in a stack of reams of bond paper. When the stock level reaches the coloured tab it is time to reorder the item.

Other visual systems may take the form of a wall chart showing the stock used.

A bin system

Loose small items are kept in appropriate sized bins or boxes. Reordering is put into effect when stock reaches a particular level, see the diagram below.

Reorder level

Both the above systems rely solely on visual checking to determine the stock position. There are no specific historical records which show exactly when, to whom and in what quantity items were issued. It would be necessary to analyse *all* requisitions to obtain a full picture of their use.

A stock card system – manual or computerised

With stock card systems records are kept for the quantity of *each* item in stock. A minimum level of stock is fixed at the point where there should be enough in hand to cover the time between the placing of the order and the receipt of that order. A maximum level is fixed at a point that ensures not too much capital or storage space is tied up in idle stock.

Stationery Stock Card

Item _Treasury Tags_
(boxes of 50) mixed colours

Maximum Stock: 40 boxes
Minimum Stock: 10 boxes

Date 199–	Receipts			Issues			Balance in Stock
	Quantity Received	Invoice No.	Supplier	Quantity Issued	Requisition No.	Department	
Jan 1							30 boxes
" 8				1 box	153	Reception	29 "
" 11				10 boxes	401	Filing dept.	19 "
March 1				8 boxes	477	Personnel dept.	11 "
" 3	25 boxes	450	Office Equipment Supplies Ltd.				36 "

Stock record card – specimen

Each item of stock has its individual stock card which clearly shows all the necessary information about the stock. Maximum and minimum levels are shown on the card. The remainder of the card is divided into two halves, one showing the receiving of supplies of new stock and the other half showing the issuing of stock to members of staff in the organisation. Some cards have an extra column to show when the stock has been reordered.

Activity 9.1.2

Prepare a stock record card for A4 White Bond Paper. There were 20 reams of the paper in stock at 1.6.9-. The maximum level is 50 reams and the minimum is 20 reams. Today (3.6.9-) you have received 30 reams from PaperBase Ltd (Invoice no. 2316) and issued 5 reams to the personnel department.

FACT FINDER

Stock control procedures

Whether the stock control system is manual or computerised a company should have an efficient procedure for the issue and control of stock. Stores of office supplies may be centralised or there may be a separate store in each department.

A stock control procedure may incorporate the following:

1 One member of staff will be responsible for the control of supplies with a named deputy in case of absence.

2 When stock is received it will be entered in a stock received book or recorded on the computer. The items will be carefully checked for quality and condition before being placed in store.

3 Stock control cards (if used) will be updated with new stock levels. This will be done automatically on most stock control software.

4 Records will be regularly checked and analysed to check for undue wastage or pilfering.

5 Store cupboards will be locked when the control clerk is not present.

6 Supplies will only be against a requisition signed by an authorised member of staff.

7 Supplies will only be issued at certain times.

8 Ordering and reordering of stock will be carried out by the person responsible for stores.

Stock requisitions

When a section or department requires items out of stores an internal requisition form will be prepared. To ensure adequate control it is usual for the signature of someone in authority to be required before stock is issued. These signatories would be known to the stock controller and s/he would not accept a request without an appropriate signature.

With such a procedure in place it is unlikely that unacceptable requests will be made.

Activity 9.1.3

Design a simple requisition form for obtaining stock from a centralised office supplies store or obtain a copy of the one used at your place of work.

Location of stock

It is important that stock should be appropriately stored. Heavy items should be near the floor with frequently used items easily accessible. Personnel dealing with stock should ensure that all items are kept dry. Using up old stock rather than issuing new items is also most important, otherwise stock may deteriorate after a lengthy storage or become out-of-date. The effect of heat on some stock, such as carbon or NCR paper, should not be forgotten.

All aspects of health and safety should be followed when storing and handling stock. There are standard procedures to be followed when lifting heavy items (see Unit 10). A trolley should be used when moving heavy stock around.

Activity 9.1.4

With reference to the location of office supplies, what other factors should be taken into account when choosing the most appropriate place for an item to be stored?

Referring to the list that you prepared in Activity 9.1.1 state, by the side of each item, which method of stock control would be most appropriate. In addition, referring to the list below, state which you consider to be the most appropriate place for the item to be placed in the store room, giving your reasons.

A   Open shelf – top
B   Open shelf – middle
C   Open shelf – bottom
D   Locked cupboard
E   Away from light
F   Away from heat

Are there any legal requirements for storing certain types of stock?

Computerised stock control programs

There are several computerised stock control programs on the market which have advantages over manual systems. For example, as soon as stock is issued stock levels and total valuations are automatically updated. At the press of a button an up-to-date print-out of all stock may be obtained. Should stock fall below minimum levels then an order may be automatically raised.

Operators of a computerised system require basic computer skills as well as an understanding of basic stock control procedures. The initial setting up of the system requires thought and knowledge of the software's capabilitites. The references for stock items need to be decided logically with all data being keyed in and checked for accuracy.

If office supplies' records are computerised they are likely to be part of the overall stock control system for the organisation.

Activity 9.1.5

Investigate a computerised stock control program and write an informal report on your findings. Was the software user friendly? What specific features did it have compared to a manual system, for example, did the program list items which had slipped below minimum level and required reordering?

Stock-taking

It is necessary to check levels of stock at regular intervals to ensure that the balances on the stock cards are correct. This is also a safeguard against items being pilfered or stock deteriorating due to inappropriate or long storage. Some companies stock-take on an annual basis. With office supplies this is more likely to be done more frequently or even continuously.

Activity 9.1.6

The company secretary of your company is concerned that too much stationery is being wasted. He has noticed, among other things, that more photocopies than required are being taken, paper clips are being thrown away and new envelopes are being used for internal mail. Overheads in the office are running at a very high level and staff have been asked for their suggestions to help reduce the stationery bill.

Put forward your suggestions, in a memo, to the company secretary.

Element 9.2 – Maintain a petty cash system

Petty cash is used for the purchase of small items. Stamps, taxi fares, tea or coffee may be financed out of petty cash. Records of purchases are kept in a petty cash book which not only stops minor entries filling up the cash book but also means that official orders do not have to be prepared.

In many offices the petty cash book is kept on an **imprest system**.

With this system the company sets an appropriate **float** amount. Whenever cash is reimbursed to members of staff a voucher is prepared giving brief details of the expenditure and signed both by the member of staff and the petty cashier.

Any member of staff claiming from petty cash should, whenever possible, obtain a VAT receipt for money spent. The vouchers and the receipts are the petty cashier's proof that the cash has been paid out of the account.

The float is regularly 'topped up' to its original amount by putting in a sum of money equal to the total value of vouchers issued during the period.

It is advisable for one member of staff to be responsible for petty cash and a cash box should be kept for the float.

FACT FINDER

Setting up and operating a petty cash account

1   Obtain a petty cash book or rule up as appropriate (see sample on page 156).

2   Decide on headings for the analysis columns. Frequently used ones are: postage, travel, stationery and office expenses and, of course, one for Valued Added Tax (VAT).

   VAT is charged in the UK on both goods and services. Some goods and services, such as food and postal charges are not liable to VAT. The present VAT rate is 17½ per cent. It is necessary to record all VAT amounts on purchases as a company liable for VAT may offset such payments against VAT collected on sales.

3   Record the float coming *in* to the account under cash received.

4   Payments *out* should only be made against production of a VAT receipt and the completion of a petty cash voucher containing the signatures of the purchaser and the member of staff authorising that purchase.

5   These payments *out* should be entered once in the cash paid column and again in the correct analysis column, separating and recording VAT as necessary.

6   Regularly balance the petty cash book to determine how much cash is left in the account. The balance is the difference between receipts and payments out.

7   Check the balance against the actual money in the cash box. If the two amounts do not balance a mistake has been made or cash is missing!

8   Inform your cashier when the float is low. The amount of money spent may then, on production of receipts, be reimbursed to the petty cash account, thus bringing the float back to its original level.

Year over top of column.

Cash received in this column.

Voucher number.

Analysis columns totalled separately.

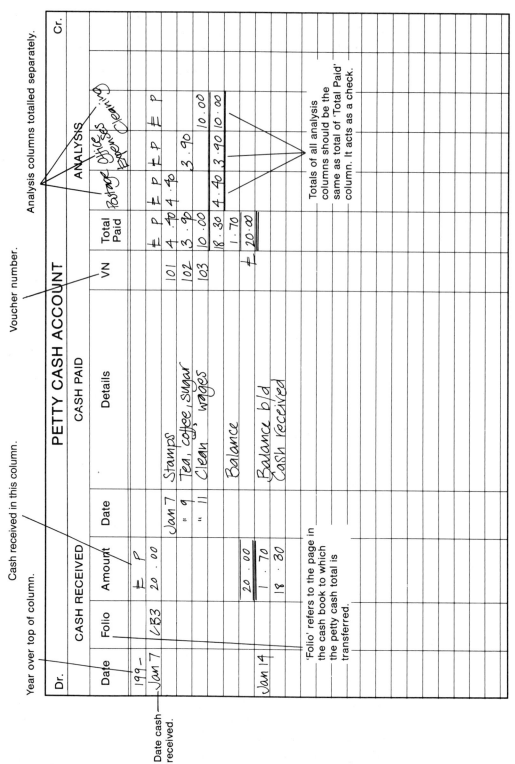

Date cash received.

'Folio' refers to the page in the cash book to which the petty cash total is transferred.

Totals of all analysis columns should be the same as total of 'Total Paid' column. It acts as a check.

PETTY CASH ACCOUNT

Dr.	CASH RECEIVED				CASH PAID				ANALYSIS			Cr.
Date	Folio	Amount		Date	Details	VN	Total Paid		Postage	Office Expenses	Cleaning	
		£	P				£	P	£ P	£ P	£ P	
199–												
Jan 7	CB3	20	00	Jan 7	Stamps	101	4	40	4 . 40			
				" 9	Tea, coffee, sugar	102	3	90		3 . 90		
				" 11	Clean, wages	103	10	00			10 . 00	
							18 . 30		4 . 40	3 . 90	10 . 00	
					Balance		1 . 70					
		20 . 00					£ 20.00					
Jan 14		1 . 70			Balance b/d							
		18 . 30			Cash received							

A petty cash account

156

Activity 9.2.1

You have just been handed the petty cash book and cash box for which you are now responsible. The person who was looking after the petty cash has gone on sick leave.

You check the money in the cash box and find that it does not agree with the balance on the account. You have been told that all was in order at the end of April. The balance is £13.77 but you have counted only £2.83 in the cash box. You find a voucher for £5.48 plus £1.00 VAT in the box which has not been entered in the book; this was for stationery. You check the items in the account to find out what has gone wrong.

Petty cash book

Receipts	Date	Details	VN	Total payments	Office exps	Travel exps	Postage	VAT
£				£	£	£	£	£
23.67	30/4	Balance b/d						
26.33	1/5	Cash						
	1/5	Milk	21	4.46				
	4/5	Postage	22	2.30			2.30	
	5/5	Taxi	23	2.35		2.00		0.35
	9/5	Milk	24	4.46	4.46			
	12/5	Windows	25	5.00	5.00			
	13/5	Coffee	26	2.80	2.80			
	14/5	Flowers	27	9.40	8.00			1.40
	18/5	Milk	28	9.92	9.92			
				36.23	30.18	2.00	2.30	1.75
	31/5	Balance c/d		13.77				
50.00				50.00				
13.77	1/6	Balance b/d						

1 Make a note of what has gone wrong with the account and adjust the figures as necessary.

2 You now have to enter up the account for the month of June. Enter the following transactions, balance the account and bring down the balance on 30 June. Restore the imprest.

			£	VAT inc £
June	2	Cash received	47.17	
	4	Postage stamps	3.40	
	5	Taxi fare	2.35	0.35
	6	Milk	4.46	
	9	Stationery	4.70	0.70
	13	Milk	4.46	
	17	Postage	1.24	
	20	Flowers	7.05	1.05
	20	Milk	4.46	
	23	Window cleaner	5.00	
	27	Milk	4.46	
	30	Tea and coffee	3.90	

Element 9.3 – Ensure the use of authorised banking procedures

Banking is a very important part of a company's financial procedures. Without the many and varied services of the banks modern business activity would virtually come to a halt.

Your employer will almost certainly have at least one bank account and as an administrative assistant you may be involved in carrying out some of the work involved. It is essential that you have a sound knowledge of basic banking procedures.

There are various documents provided by the main clearing banks to ensure that certain information required is provided in a banking transaction. You should be aware of their purpose and use in a banking transaction.

Some of the documents you may be asked to handle are paying-in slips, standing orders and direct debits, bank drafts, cheques and bank statements. Illustrations of some of these documents are given below together with information on the data to be recorded on the document.

FACT FINDER

It is vitally important to record all information correctly onto banking forms and to double-check data written on documents either by you or your junior.

The specimen banking documents, together with their text, reproduced on the following pages are by kind permission of Lloyds Bank Plc, 1991.

Specimen completed cheque

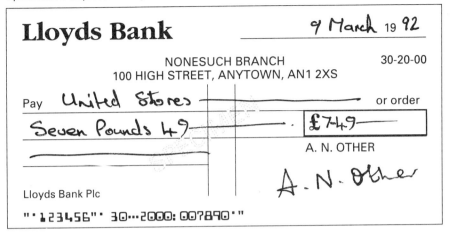

When preparing a cheque

1   Always write in ink or ball-point pen – *never* pencil.

2   Write out the amount of the cheque in both words and figures – this gives the bank a double-check on the amount you want to be paid and prevents your cheques being altered (particularly the figures).

3   Draw lines through any unused spaces (so that no one can add anything to the amount you want to pay out).

4   Sign your cheque with your usual signature.

5   Do not forget to make a note of the cheque details on the special pages or stubs provided in the cheque book – this will be your record of what you have paid out, to whom and when.

6   Crossings – all cheque books issued are 'crossed' which gives extra protection. If an 'open' cheque fell into the hands of a dishonest person, s/he might take it to the bank and obtain cash for it. If your cheque is 'crossed' then it has to be paid into a bank account.

For regular payments to be made under a Standing Order (S/O) or Direct Debit (D/D) it is necessary to contact your bank and complete the necessary forms. Some establishments, for example, electricity boards and local councils, will provide their own forms for customers to complete. The form will contain full details about the payment giving the amount, name and account of person or company receiving payment, and dates for payments to commence and end. An example of a standing order mandate is shown on page 160.

159

Example of standing order mandate

AUTHORITY 12 (1978) Standing Order Mandate
TO LLOYDS BANK PLC

Address _____

	Bank	Branch Title (not address)	Sorting Code Number
Please pay			— —
		Beneficiary's Name	Account Number
for the credit of			

	Regular amount in figures	Regular amount in words
the sum of	£	

	Date and Amount of First Payment		Due Date and Frequency
commencing	*NOW £	and thereafter every	
	Date and Amount of Last Payment		
*until	£	*until you receive further notice from me/us in writing	
quoting the reference		and debit my/our account accordingly.	

This instruction cancels any previous order in favour of the beneficiary named above, under this reference.

Special instructions:

Account to be Debited	Account Number

Signature(s) _____   Date _____

_____

Note: The Bank will not undertake to:
     (i)   make any reference to Value Added Tax or other indeterminate element,
     (ii)   advise payer's address to beneficiary,
     (iii) advise beneficiary of inability to pay,
     (iv) request beneficiary's banker to advise beneficiary of receipt of payment.

*Delete if not applicable

A **banker's draft** is a way of paying out larger amounts of money to individuals and organisations abroad. The draft is similar to a cheque but drawn by the bank on an overseas branch and made payable to a third party. This way the payee is guaranteed payment either in sterling or in a foreign currency.

Specimen bank giro credit slip

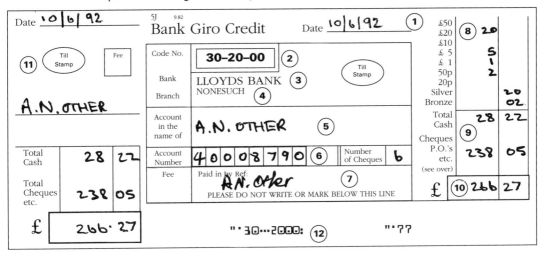

The numbers refer to the points set out below:

1 Date.
2 Sorting code number of the account holding branch.
3 Name of account holding bank.
4 Name of account holding branch.
5 Account holder's name.
6 Account number.
7 Signature of person paying the money in.
8 Breakdown of cash paid in.
9 Total of cheques paid in, details of which are listed on the back.
10 Total of the credit to the account (cash and cheques).
11 Counterfoil (your record of what you have paid in).
12 Magnetic ink symbols to enable automatic processing by the computer.

Banking services

A bank offers a whole range of services to its customers. In addition to the various accounts, cash, debit and credit card facilities, the main banks also offer such services as advice on investments and insurance. They will also act as executors to wills, provide a safe deposit box for valuables and a night safe for those who wish to lodge cash and cheques at the bank outside normal working hours.

Bank services for travellers

The commercial banks will arrange for amounts of foreign cash to be available on order. However this is not a very safe way for business people to carry their money when abroad. The widespread acceptance of **credit cards**, for example, American Express and Eurocard means the traveller has a much safer and easier way of making payments.

Another safe way to provide personal finance whilst abroad is to purchase travellers' cheques. These can be purchased in denominations of £2, £5, £10, £20 and £50, or in other currencies, such as American dollars or Spanish pesetas, if this is more convenient. When travellers' cheques are bought the user is required to sign the cheque. When the cheque is cashed the user is required to sign the cheque again in the presence of the cashier. Travellers' cheques will sometimes be accepted as direct payment at garages, restaurants and retail outlets.

Travellers' cheques have reference numbers and the purchaser should ensure this information is kept in a safe place in case the cheques are stolen. The purchaser may then be reimbursed with the lost amount (see also Unit 4).

Specimen Bank Statement

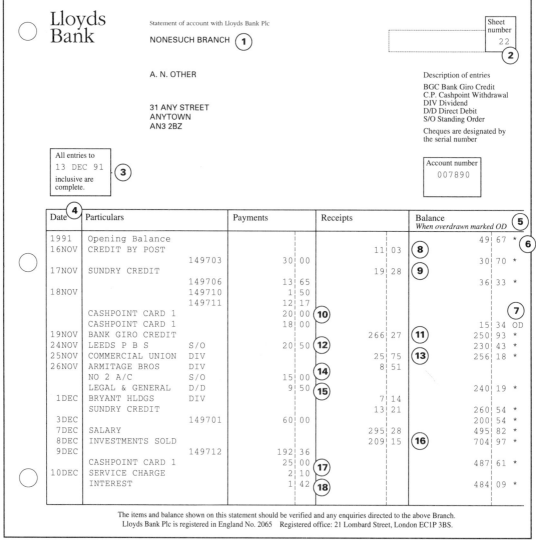

1 Name of the account holding branch.
2 Statement number.
3 Date on which the statement is produced.

4   Date on which account has been debited or credited for each transaction.
5   Balance on the account after day's transactions have been completed.
6   Symbol denoting credit balance.
7   Symbol denoting overdrawn balance.
8   Items received by post for the credit of customer's account.
9   Credits paid in at customer's own bank branch.
10   Entry denoting withdrawal, using the bank's Cashpoint machine (an automated cash dispenser).
11   Credits paid in at another bank or branch, either by the customer or by a third party (other than salary).
12   Standing Order – regular payment made automatically by the bank in accordance with customer's instructions.
13   Dividend – credit received from a company representing income earned from the customer's shares.
14   Regular payments made by standing order to repay customer's loan from the bank.
15   Direct debit – a regular payment like a standing order, but payment is originated by the named company. The bank holds the customer's instructions to debit the account.
16   Entry denoting investments (eg shares) sold by the bank for the customer, under her/his instructions.
17   Bank charge levied for operating the account during the quarterly period September 1991 to December 1991.
18   Interest charge levied on any overdrawn balance on the account during the quarterly period September 1991 to December 1991.

Activity 9.3.1

Building societies also provide financial services for their customers. Investigate a local branch of a well-known building society and find out what particular services they offer.

Terminology

A knowledge of certain terms will also be of great use to you.

FACT FINDER

Some basic banking terms

Payee – The person/company who is to receive payment. On a cheque this refers to the name the cheque is made out to.

Payer/drawer – The person/company who is making payment; the one who is signing the cheque.

Drawee – The bank on which a cheque is drawn

Asset – Something you or the company owns which is of value.

Liability – A payment that is due by you or the company; something that is owed.

163

Debtor – The person/company that owes money; classed as an asset for the one owed the money.

Creditor – The person/company to whom we owe money; classed as a liability for the one who owes money.

The handling of cash and postal orders, alongside banking forms, may also be part of your involvement with banking procedures. When dealing with any of these items always ensure that money and forms are not left lying on desks and cash and cheques are locked away in a safe when not required.

Frequently, the information being dealt with is of a confidential nature and great care should be taken to ensure that unauthorised staff or visitors do not have access to such data. It may be the latest bank statement of a local company or the credit schedule for the payment of staff salaries that is left lying in full view on the desk.

Activity 9.3.2

You work for a firm of accountants and handle a whole range of financial documents. You now have an assistant to help you with your work. S/he is concerned about the confidentiality and security aspects of her/his new job and has asked you for help.

Set out guidelines to help your new assistant deal with all matters of confidentiality and security which may present themselves in her/his new post.

Bank reconciliation

At regular intervals the bank will send the company a statement listing the numbers of all the items, for example, cheques and direct debits which have been deducted from the balance of your account and all the amounts that have been added (credit transfers, sundry credits to the balance of your account, etc).

You may be asked to **reconcile** the bank statement with the company's own record. The preparation of a bank reconciliation statement is to 'agree' the balance on the bank statement with the balance in the company's cash book. Usually, at first sight, these balances do not agree. Frequently it is just a matter of timing which creates the difference rather than that an error has been made. Other reasons could be that:

1 Your company may have handed cheques in payment to creditors (persons to whom they owe money) but the payees have not yet presented them to their banks for payment.

2 Credit transfers and direct debits may have been processed through your

company's account at the bank, but as yet do not appear in your company's books.

3 Items such as bank charges and bank interest may not be known until the bank statement is received.

You must first appreciate that receipts in your company's records appear as debits whilst on the bank statement receipts appear as credits. Likewise, payments out from the company appear as credits in your records and debits on the bank statement. This is because the statement is prepared from the bank's view of their transactions with you.

How to reconcile statements (manual)

1 With the documents in front of you tick off the items which are identical.

2 From the two documents it can then be seen where the discrepancies are.

3 You should first bring the cash book up-to-date by entering in any items shown on the bank statement, but not in the cash book.

4 Now prepare the bank reconciliation statement. You may start with either the bank statement balance or the cash book balance. For convenience we will start with the bank statement balance.

You must *add* those items to the final bank balance which have been debited to your cash book, but which have not been credited to the bank statement.

You must *deduct* those items from the bank balance which have been credited to your cash book but which have not been debited to the bank statement.

The cash book balance calculated in step 3 should *equal* that prepared in step 4.

Bank statement

Date 199-	Details		Dr £	Cr £	Balance £
1 July	Opening balance				1205.50 CR
3 July	J Strange	223421	12.40		1193.10 CR
5 July	R Tiptree	223422	108.54		1084.56 CR
8 July	Standard Ins	D/D	34.00		1050.56 CR
12 July	Ronstone	BGC		198.75	1249.31 CR
19 July	Altons	S/O	10.00		1239.31 CR
23 July	Ropers	BGC		342.80	1582.11 CR
26 July	Preston	BGC		100.30	1682.41 CR

Cash book

Date 199-	Details		Dr £	Cr £	Balance £
1 July	Opening balance				1205.50 DR
1 July	J Strange	223421		12.40	1193.10 DR
1 July	R Tiptree	223422		108.54	1084.56 DR
1 July	L Netherton	223423		120.00	964.56 DR
13 July	Ronstone	BGC	198.75		1163.31 DR
19 July	Altons	S/O		10.00	1153.31 DR
20 July	Standard Ins	D/D		34.00	1119.31 DR
26 July	Ropers	BGC	342.80		1462.11 DR
28 July	Preston	BGC	100.30		1562.41 DR
30 July	Crawley	C/C	130.00		1692.41 DR

Bank reconciliation statement as at 31 July 199-

	£
Balance as per bank statement	1682.41
Add counter credit not yet entered on bank statement	130.00
	1812.40
Less unpresented cheque	
Netherton 223423	120.00
Balance as per cash book	1692.41

In this instance the cash book did not need amending.

Activity 9.3.4

Bring the cash book up-to-date and state the new balance at

31 May 199-. Prepare a statement reconciling the difference between the new up-to-date balance in the cash book and the balance on the bank statement.

Bank statement

Date 199-	Details		Dr £	Cr £	Balance £
1 May	Opening balance				211.44 CR
5 May	Carter	BGC		200.00	411.44 CR
5 May	Lemon	124421	9.18		402.26 CR
8 May	Baxter	124423	29.42		372.84 CR
15 May	Stone	124425	98.17		274.67 CR
19 May	Marrett	BGC		259.00	535.67 CR
24 May	MEB	DD	79.00		454.67 CR
26 May	Severn Trent	SO	50.00		404.67 CR
26 May	Pearson	124426	23.56		381.11 CR

Cash book (bank columns only)

Date 199-	Details		Dr £	Cr £	Balance £
1 May	Opening balance				211.44 CR
3 May	Lemon	124421		9.18	202.26 CR
3 May	Turner	124422		43.34	158.92 CR
3 May	Baxter	124423		29.42	129.50 CR
3 May	Saxon	124424		87.45	42.05 CR
8 May	Carter	BGC	200.00		242.05 CR
9 May	Stone	124425		98.17	143.88 CR
23 May	Marrett	BGC	259.00		402.88 CR
25 May	MEB	DD		79.00	323.88 CR
25 May	Pearson	124426		23.56	300.32 CR

Accounting errors

There may be occasions when a mistake has been made either by your company or the bank. Depending on your position in the company, you should contact your chief cashier or accountant and point the matter out to her/him. Any error is, of course, likely to be apparent from your reconciliation statement.

UNIT

9

Work-related tasks

One of your jobs as an administrative assistant at The Westlands holiday centre is to be in charge of the stationery stock. The stationery was solely for use in the centre's offices but recently there has been a change of policy so that now there are direct sales of stationery items to customers and clients through the centre's retail outlet.

Requirements have increased considerably during the last few weeks and you are finding it difficult to cope with the present informal system of stock control.

You have recently had to take stock of what is actually in the store and you have added details of the cost and selling prices, plus a maximum and minimum level that has been set, for each item (see list of items in stock at 30 June 199- on page 169). Until you implemented this stock-take you had no other means of identifying the levels of stock.

TASK ONE – Elements 9.1 and 9.3

You receive the following memo. Deal with it as a matter of urgency.

M E M O R A N D U M

From: John Davies, Centre Accountant

TO: You (Administrative Assistant)

DATE: 2 July 1992

STATIONERY STOCK

Please would you let me have as soon as possible an accurate total valuation of stationery stock. List all the items showing individual cost values plus the total.

I need this figure urgently for preparation of our final accounts.

Many thanks.

You decide to give the calculation work to your assistant. Whilst the task is being carried out check your assistant's progress and when completed check the accuracy. Send a reply memo to the centre accountant giving the correct information.

List of items in stock at 30 June 199-

Item	Quantity in stock	Cost price £ (per unit)	Selling price £ (per unit)	Max level	Min level
Adhesive tape	10 rolls	0.80	1.20	10	7
Bank paper (white)	5 reams	1.10	1.65	12	4
Bank paper (yellow)	10 reams	1.10	1.65	12	4
Bank paper (blue)	11 reams	1.10	1.65	12	4
Biros (black)	13	0.28	0.42	30	10
Biros (blue)	25	0.28	0.42	30	10
Biros (red)	20	0.28	0.42	30	10
Biros (green)	14	0.28	0.42	30	10
Bond paper (white)	10 reams	1.20	1.80	12	4
Bond paper (yellow)	12	1.20	1.80	12	4
Bond paper (blue)	12	1.20	1.80	12	4
Brown paper	20 sheets	0.35	0.52	24	8
Bulldog clips	15	0.56	0.84	20	10
Correcting fluid	6 bottles	0.65	0.98	12	2
Document wallets	50	0.20	0.30	60	20
Elastic bands	3 boxes	1.20	1.80	5	2
Envelopes DL white	6 packs	1.40	2.10	12	2
Envelopes DL brown	12 packs	1.10	1.65	12	2
Envelopes C6 white	10 packs	1.20	1.80	12	2
Envelopes C6 brown	12 packs	1.05	1.58	12	2
Folders (square cut)	60	0.20	0.30	60	20
Glue	10 sticks	0.60	0.90	12	2
Memo pads	8 pads	1.60	2.40	10	2
Paper clips (small)	5 boxes	1.40	2.10	6	2
Paper clips (large)	6 Boxes	1.50	2.25	6	2
Pencils (HB)	40	0.08	0.12	50	10
Pins	2 boxes	0.40	0.60	4	1
Telephone pads	4 pads	1.30	1.95	8	2
Treasury tags	5 boxes	1.10	1.65	6	2
Staples (56)	8 boxes	2.20	3.30	10	4
String	4 balls	1.60	2.40	6	2

TASK TWO – Element 9.1

You have had informal discussions with various members of staff concerning the need for a more efficient method of controlling the stationery supply.

You receive the following memo.

MEMORANDUM

FROM: Graham Allen, Company Secretary

TO: You (Administrative Assistant)

DATE: 2 July 199-

STATIONERY STOCK

Further to our recent discussion concerning bringing in new control procedures for office supplies please investigate this further and let me have your ideas on the subject in writing. Set out your findings in an informal report (see Unit 5).

We have an Executive Committee meeting a week today and I would like to present your report to the team. There is very little cash for such a venture so keep the system as inexpensive and simple as possible. We may be able to look at a computerised system next year.

Send your reply to Mr Allen in the form of a memo setting out your ideas for a new stock control system, giving details of the procedures necessary to be set up for it to run smoothly.

TASK THREE – Elements 9.1 and 9.2

A few days later you receive the following requisition from the retail outlet:

STATIONERY REQUISTION

No:

Section: Date:

Quantity	Description
20	HB Pencils
10 sticks	Glue
6 packs	White Envelopes (DL)

Signed: ...... *P. Lewis* ...... Store Control Clerk

Authorised by ...... *L Jackson* ......

You are not sure whether this requisition can be met and you check your stock list. In fact you can just meet the requisition, but are now completely out of two items – glue and white envelopes, size DL.

1 You decide to send your junior to buy these items out of petty cash so that you will be able to fulfil any other request that comes along.

   Your junior knows nothing about petty cash so you decide to set out guidelines on an information sheet for her/him.

2   It is 5 July 199- and on checking your stock records you realise that the minimum and maximum levels for some items are unrealistic and need adjusting (see list of items in stock at 5 July 199-, below). Change them as necessary and print out a revised list of items.

3   Prepare an appropriate purchase requistion for the centre buyer.

List of items in stock at 5 July 199-

Item	Quantity in stock	Cost price £ (per unit)	Selling price £ (per unit)	Max level	Min level
Adhesive tape	10 rolls	0.80	1.20	10	7
Bank paper (white)	4 reams	1.10	1.65	12	4
Bank paper (yellow)	10 reams	1.10	1.65	12	4
Bank paper (blue)	11 reams	1.10	1.65	12	4
Biros (black)	8	0.28	0.42	30	10
Biros (blue)	25	0.28	0.42	30	10
Biros (red)	20	0.28	0.42	30	10
Biros (green)	14	0.28	0.42	30	10
Bond paper (white)	4 reams	1.20	1.80	12	4
Bond paper (yellow)	12	1.20	1.80	12	4
Bond paper (blue)	12	1.20	1.80	12	4
Brown paper	20 sheets	0.35	0.52	24	8
Bulldog clips	15	0.56	0.84	20	10
Correcting fluid	6 bottles	0.65	0.98	12	2
Document wallets	50	0.20	0.30	60	20
Elastic bands	3 boxes	1.20	1.80	5	2
Envelopes DL white	0 packs	1.40	2.10	12	2
Envelopes DL brown	12 packs	1.10	1.65	12	2
Envelopes C6 white	4 packs	1.20	1.80	12	2
Envelopes C6 brown	12 packs	1.05	1.58	12	2
Folders (square cut)	60	0.20	0.30	60	20
Glue	0 sticks	0.60	0.90	12	2
Memo pads	2 pads	1.60	2.40	10	2
Paper clips (small)	5 boxes	1.40	2.10	6	2
Paper clips (large)	6 Boxes	1.50	2.25	6	2
Pencils (HB)	20	0.08	0.12	50	10
Pins	2 boxes	0.40	0.60	4	1
Telephone pads	3 pads	1.30	1.95	8	2
Treasury tags	5 boxes	1.10	1.65	6	2
Staples (56)	6 boxes	2.20	3.30	10	4
String	4 balls	1.60	2.40	6	2

■ TASK FOUR – Element 9.3

1 The retail outlet has run out of small change and you have been asked to collect £200 of change from the bank. Draw up an appropriate cash analysis of the coinage to be collected (£1, 50p, 20p,10p, 5p, 2p and 1p) and prepare a cheque for signature by the centre accountant.

2 What special security precautions would you take when coming back to the company from the bank?

3 Several days later you are asked to fill in some banking documents:

a) A standing order to be made payable to Meridan Property Services for £300.00 per month for the rent on some offices the centre is using. The order is to last for a year and the amount is to be paid on the 15th of each month. The centre's bank is Lloyds Bank PLC at their Colchester Branch, account number 01187389. Meridan Property Services bank at the Colchester Midland Bank, account number 11889924.

b) A paying-in slip for the following cash and cheques:

$43 \times £20.00$, $23 \times £10$, $38 \times £5.00$;

cheques for £15.00 and £78.50 from R. Walters and Thornes PLC respectively.

Make sure you fill in all the details on the documents and add up the totals as necessary.

4 Your junior asks you why the company pays some creditors by direct debit. What is the difference when compared with a standing order? Set out your answer on a fact sheet.

Health and safety at work

Main elements covered

10.1   Monitor and maintain health and safety within the work area

Supplementary elements covered

2.3   Organise and present information in a variety of formats

5.1   Produce text from oral and written material using an alphanumeric keyboard

5.2   Present narrative, graphic and tabular information using an alphanumeric keyboard

Element 10.1 – Monitor and maintain health and safety within the work area

A pleasant and well-laid out office, free from hazards, contributes to developing a happy and well-motivated work-force. Whilst there are many pleasant modern offices around there are still a number which do not meet minimum standards.

In the past, there was little legislation to improve the conditions and working environment of the office worker. Now there are legal minimum standards for space, lighting, heating, ventilation, cleanliness, etc. In addition, far more research has been carried out to improve the relationship between the design of the equipment and comfort and productivity of the workers who use it.

The provision of safe working conditions and the prevention of accidents is most important. Employees and employers are obliged to protect their own health and safety and those of others who may be affected by their behaviour at work.

Activity 10.1.1

How safety conscious are you? What do you know about your legal or moral responsibilities?

Answer the following questions *truthfully*.

1   Is there anything that you do at work which creates a hazard to other people?

2 Do you believe that you should take reasonable care at work because:
   a) It is in your own interest?
   b) You might otherwise cause injury to other people?
   c) You are legally expected to do so?

3 Would you recognise the alarm signal to evacuate the buildings where you work and/or study?

4 Do you know *how* to raise the alarm should there be an emergency in the building where you work and/or study?

5 Do you know *who* would take care of disabled people in these buildings, in the event of an emergency?

6 Do you know the emergency escape routes in the buildings where you work and/or study?

7 In the event of a fire would you know how to use a fire extinguisher and *which* one to use?

8 What action should you take on finding a fault in electrical equipment which appears to make it unsafe?

9 Do you know the names of any trained first aiders at your place of work or study? Do you know how or where to contact them should there be an emergency?

10 Do you know what procedure to follow if you or your colleagues have an accident at work?

If you were able to answer all these questions – well done! If you answered 'Don't know' to most of them you are *not* very safety conscious.

Health and safety legislation

Whilst many offices today are well-planned, pleasant and safe places in which to work, this was not always the case. The change in attitude to health and safety in the office is mainly due to the three important Acts of Parliament.

- The Health and Safety at Work, etc Act 1974;

- The Offices, Shops and Railway Premises Act 1963; and

- The Fire Precautions Act 1971.

When the Health and Safety at Work, etc Act was passed in 1974, for the first time the responsibilities of employees as well as employers was spelt out. An employee now has a responsibility for her/his own health and safety and for that of other persons who may be affected by her/his actions.

FACT FINDER

Health and Safety at Work, etc Act 1974

Employee's responsibilities

Every employee has a duty while at work:

1 To take reasonable care for the health and safety of her/himself and of other persons who may be affected by her/his acts or omissions at work; and

2 To co-operate with her/his employers so far as is necessary to enable them to fulfil any statutory duty or requirement to be performed or complied with under this Act.

Employer's responsibilities

Every employer has a duty to ensure the health, safety and welfare at work of all her/his employees so far as is reasonably practicable. This responsibility will include, in particular:

1 The provision and maintenance of plant and systems of work that are, so far as is reasonably practicable, safe and without risks to health.

2 Arrangements for ensuring, so far as is reasonably practicable, safety and absence of risks to health in connection with the use, handling, storage and transport of articles and substances.

3 The provision of such instruction, training and supervision as is necessary to ensure, so far as is reasonably practicable, the health and safety at work of her/his employees.

4 So far as is reasonably practicable, as regards any place of work under the employer's control, its maintenance in a condition that is safe and without risks to health and the provision and maintenance of means of access to and exits from it that are safe and without such risks.

5 The provision and maintenance of a working environment for her/his employees that is, so far as is reasonably practicable, safe, without risks to health, and adequate as regards facilities and arrangements for employees' welfare at work.

In addition, the Act states that an employer who has five or more employees must prepare a written statement of her/his general policy on health and safety at work for her/his employees, together with the organisation and arrangements that are in force for carrying out that policy and bringing it to the notice of her/his employees. Employers should consult with representatives of the employees concerning these arrangements to ensure effective co-operation in promoting and developing health and safety at their place of work.

Activity 10.1.2

Your director has recently noticed a slackness amongst your staff with regard to health and safety. S/he was particularly anxious when s/he saw a young member of staff attempting to move a heavy electronic typewriter. S/he has asked you to draft a memo to be sent out to all staff reminding them of their legal responsibilities and giving instances where lack of regard for health and safety is leading to a potentially dangerous and unhealthy environment. Give some specific advice on carrying heavy items.

Accidents at work

If an employee has an accident at work it must be recorded for any possible negligent claim in the future. If no record is prepared, employees may lose their right to social security industrial injury benefit. In extreme cases, the employee might sue the company, so accurate records are essential evidence.

Below is an example of a simple accident form.

Staff accident report form

Name of injured person ....

Age .... Occupation ....

Home address ....

Department in which employed ....

Date of accident .... Time of accident ....

Location of accident ....

Details of injuries ....

....

Details of treatment ....

Names of witnesses ....

Signature .... Date................................

FACT
FINDER

An accident record must show:

1 The full name, address and occupation of the injured employee.

2 The date and time of the accident.

3 The place where the accident occurred.

4 The cause and nature of the injury.

5 The name, address and occupation of the person who has completed the accident record.

If an accident on the employer's premises results in the death of, or major injury to, any person then the employer must immediately inform the Local Authority Health and Safety Inspector. The employer must maintain a written record of all such accidents.

Activity 10.1.3

At 2.30 pm approximately on 12 June 199- Sharon Preece fell over a trailing flex from a computer in the accounts office, twisting her ankle and badly bruising the right side of her face when she fell onto a filing cabinet. The company nurse administered first aid and bandaged the ankle before Sharon was taken to the local hospital casualty department for an X-ray. Sharon did not return to work for two days. The accident was witnessed by two men in accounts and the chief cashier, Mrs Patel.

You are asked to complete the accident report form relating to this incident. You find out from the personnel department that Sharon was born on 2nd April 1961 and lives at 65 Hawkes Avenue, Stoke Newington, London, N16.

Lifting heavy items without due care is one of the main causes of injuries in the office. Very heavy equipment and materials should always be moved using a trolley. If the article is comparatively light and may be carried reasonably easily the carrier should follow the rules given below.

FACT
FINDER

1 Stand near to the item to be lifted.

2 Place feet firmly on the floor and slightly apart.

3 Keeping your back straight, bend your knees and pick up the item to be carried.

4 If the item is a typewriter, or any other object with an uneven distribution of weight, ensure that the heavy part is closest to your body.

5 Take care when you are carrying items that you have a clear view ahead and the item does not obstruct your vision in any way.

Other hazards in the office are many and varied. They may include trailing flexes from electrical equipment, newly washed and wet floors, bags left out in office gangways, poorly maintained electrical equipment and careless disposal of cigarette ends. In addition, staff may not be taking due notice of guidelines to ensure their own well-being, such as not adjusting the brightness on a VDU screen to suit or mis-handling the moving of equipment.

Fire is an extremely dangerous hazard, not just for the safety of staff and premises but for the continuation of the business if valuable documents and information are lost.

There are various types of fire extinguisher and it is advisable for office staff to be aware of the particular type required for, say, computer equipment.

Fire fighting equipment

In case there is a fire it is useful to know how to operate the different fire extinguishers. There is no time to read the instructions when faced with a fire. Some companies give their staff training in the use of fire fighting equipment on their induction course.

Below are listed some of the most common, portable fire extinguishers together with their distinguishing colours. It is always vitally important that the correct fire extinguisher is used.

FACT FINDER

Fire extinguishers

(The following information has been kindly supplied by the West Midlands Fire Service.)

WATER – RED

Suitable for most fires except those involving flammable liquids or live electrical apparatus.

CARBON DIOXIDE (CO$_2$) – BLACK

Suitable for fires involving flammable liquids or electrical apparatus.

FOAM – YELLOW

Suitable for most fires involving flammable liquids.

HALON – GREEN

Suitable for fires involving flammable liquids or electrical apparatus.

Halon extinguishers should not be used in confined spaces where there is a danger that the fumes may be inhaled.

DRY POWDER – BLUE

Suitable for fires involving flammable liquids or electrical apparatus.

WATER

CARBON DIOXIDE

FOAM

HALON

DRY POWDER

Fire extinguishers

When fighting a fire involving electrical equipment, first switch off the current.

It is the duty of the health and safety officer to arrange for fire extinguishers to be checked regularly to ensure that they are in good working order.

Activity 10.1.4

Your director is most concerned about fire hazards in the office. He has asked you to prepare a notice to employees warning them of the dangers of fire and bringing to their attention such points as 'Fire exits must always be kept clear' and 'Fire doors must *not* under any circumstances be locked'.

S/he wants you to include a section on the company's fire drill – what action employees should take in the event of a fire. Make the notice as eye-catching as possible. Use a desk-top publishing package, if available.

The working environment

The Offices, Shops and Railways Premises Act 1963 covers the working office environment.

FACT FINDER

The main provisions under the Act are:

1 Rooms must be adequately ventilated and lit and the temperature must reach at least 16°C (60.8°F) after the first hour of opening.

2 The average space for each office worker must be at least 3.7 m² (40 ft²) or where the ceiling is lower than 10 ft, 11 m² (400 ft³).

3 The office buildings and furniture must be cleaned regularly with floors and passages being kept safe and free from obstructions and slippery surfaces.

4 Toilet and washing facilies must be provided in adequate numbers depending upon the number of people working on the premises.

5 Drinking water must be available.

6 First aid box(es) must be provided and properly maintained.

7 Staff must be protected from dangerous machinery.

8 No worker should be expected to lift or carry loads heavy enough to cause injury.

Activity 10.1.5

First aid

As stated in the Offices, Shops and Railway Premises Act 1963 a first aid box must be provided for the use of staff and be readily accessible to them. The contents must be replenished frequently and the name and location of named, qualified first aiders should be clearly displayed.

Check the first aid box at your place of work and/or study and make a list of the items contained inside. Find out the names and locations of the establishment's qualified first aiders.

Ergonomics

Ergonomics is the study of the relationship between the design of office equipment and the comfort and productivity of those who use it. Well-designed offices and equipment reduce fatigue and discomfort.

Visual Display Units (VDUs)

The arrival of the computer, whilst bringing many advantages to companies, has also brought certain health and safety problems. Operators may develop eyestrain and backache. Whilst there is no firm evidence that health is permanently damaged by using VDUs it is advisable to limit the time spent at a computer. This is especially relevant to those people who suffer from such disorders as migraine and epilepsy. There have also been some reports that the radiation from VDUs is harmful to the unborn child. Whilst this is not certain some companies will offer pregnant women alternative employment during their pregnancies.

Repetitive Strain Injury (RSI) is a term used to describe the medical condition which some VDU users may experience after spending lengthy periods working at a keyboard. Apart from painful arm and shoulder joints, sufferers may also experience tingling in the fingers.

Recently, two consultative documents have been published by the Health and Safety Commission which contain proposals for implementing the European Community Directive on Display Screen Equipment. Free eye tests and regular breaks for users are included in the proposals for those staff who use display screen equipment for a significant part of their normal work.

In the meantime, it is suggested that due care is taken at all times to ensure that all possible harmful effects are minimised.

FACT FINDER

Good ergonomic practice involves obeying the following rules:

The screen

The operator must adjust the screen to suit her/himself both for contrast and brightness, and ensure that it is at the correct height and tilt to give a clear view of the screen's contents.

181

Take care when choosing the colour of the screen display when buying a new VDU. The colours differ depending on the manufacturer. Green, black, white and amber are the main colours used for characters, with green and amber being considered to be the most restful on the eyes. Coloured monitors are capable of changing the background and character colour as required.

Use an anti-reflective screen if possible. Such screens are now produced as standard by some manufacturers. Otherwise an anti-reflective device can be fitted over an existing screen to reduce the problem of glare.

Note: Some trade unions have negotiated regular breaks from the screen for their VDU operators. One union has an agreement which specifies 100 minutes maximum per day at the screen whilst another has an agreement that there should be a 20 minute break in every two-hour period at the screen.

The keyboard

Use a detachable keyboard. In the past, computer keyboards and screens were housed together in one unit; nowadays most keyboards are detachable thus allowing plenty of scope for changing the distance of the operator from the screen. The tilt on some keyboards may be adjusted, giving further flexibility to ensure comfort.

Cable management

Ensure that trailing flexes do not prove a hazard. Most custom-built computer furniture has special slots for printer and VDU cables.

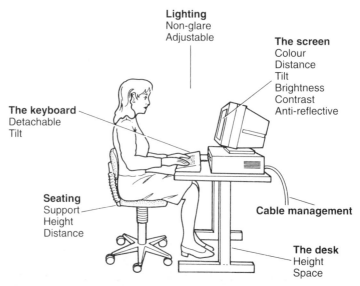

The main factors to consider when setting up a work station

Seating

Use properly designed chairs which help prevent any problem from backache and joint injury. However it is most important that the operator sits in the chair properly in relation to the screen and the keyboard!

The desk

Have the desk at the correct height and provide enough surface space for the operator to work.

Lighting

Have adjustable lights so that the desk top is well lit and there is no glare. Traditional ceiling lighting tends to give rise to glare.

Work-related task

TASK ONE – Element 10.1

The firm of Rich & Broke (solicitors) rent the third and fourth floors of an old-fashioned building in the city of London. In addition, they have just started to rent a new, open-plan office a few streets away. A total of 48 staff share the accommodation in the old building whilst only 24 members of staff have been allocated to share the accommodation in the new block.

This difference in office conditions for the staff has led to workers complaining to Mr Rich, the senior partner. The staff claim that the firm is contravening legislation on a number of points and gives a list of these to Mr Rich.

The next day you receive the following memo from Mr Rich.

M E M O R A N D U M

FROM: S Rich

TO: You (Administrative Assistant to Mr Rich)

DATE: 30 June 1992

OFFICE CONDITIONS

Yesterday I was handed the attached memo from staff asking for changes to health and safety practices in the company and complaining about the conditions at the old building. I need you to find out information on the

183

points below so I can deal with the matter in the next couple of days.

Safety Representatives

The staff have asked for safety representatives from each section to be elected so that a proper Health and Safety Committee may be formed. Whilst I believe this would be useful find out and clarify the company's legal position.

First Aid

Contact the local branch of the Red Cross or some other suitable contact you may have, and find out what would be the most appropriate training programme for us. Please write out some brief notes on this matter.

Would you also look at the other complaints on the list for me and find out: a) whether in fact the firm has a statutory duty to remedy these grievances; and b) if so, what action we should or could take.

Please *draft* a memo to all staff setting out the company's position and asking for volunteers both for safety representatives and staff willing to train as first aiders. If we have more than one nominee for safety representative from a section then a vote will be held.

Will you treat this matter with the utmost urgency and let me have your findings as soon as possible and at the latest by Friday 4 July 199-. I am most anxious that this matter should be resolved quickly. The whole situation is affecting staff morale.

(attached memo)

M E M O R A N D U M

TO: The Management

FROM: Members of staff at the old building

DATE: 28 June 199-

HEALTH AND SAFETY AT RICH & BROKE

We are most concerned at the poor standard of health and safety in this firm. Listed below are some of the problems the staff are facing.

1   The first aid boxes on both floors of the old

building need replacing, their hinges are broken and the supplies inside are grubby and old. Since Joe Haynes retired and Gita Sharda went to work in the new building there are no qualified first aiders working on these premises.

2   Something needs to be done about the General Office. The staff there work in overcrowded conditions. The installation of the new computer and photocopying equipment has meant there is little space left in which to work.

3   We want a review of 'Cleaning'. All the women complain about the dirty toilets and a lack of clean drinking water.

4   The noise and fumes from the road are affecting the health of all staff. In particular, we have two asthmatics who frequently are off sick. They claim their condition is worsened by the situation.

     We also have two people off sick at the moment from lifting too many heavy boxes of stationery and supplies up two flights of stairs.

5   Something needs to be done about the heating. Everyone is always complaining about it being either too hot or too cold. It's never right!

6   We are most concerned that the management are not taking any notice of complaints. One of the Telephonists recently complained about the bad carpeting in reception and reported that a client almost had a very nasty accident. Three months later nothing has been done about the situation.

We request that a Safety Committee, composed of representatives from each Department and from management, should be set up to look into all aspects of health and safety at this firm.

Shorthand transcription (optional)

Main elements covered

11.1 Product documents from shorthand notes using an alphanumeric keyboard

It would be expected that any person working to achieve competence in this unit would have already reached the required speed and theory standard.

Element 11.1 – Produce documents from shorthand notes using an alphanumeric keyboard

For this unit you will be expected to:

take notes from dictation at a minimum speed of 100 words per minute and transcribe error-free documents of at least 600 words within a one-hour working period.

Any note-taking system may be used.

FACT FINDER

When taking dictation

1 Before taking dictation always make sure that you have sufficient sharp pencils to hand or that your pen is fully inked.

2 Make sure that there are enough pages in your shorthand notebook to hold the forthcoming dictation.

3 It is advisable that if you work for more than one executive you have separate notebooks for each.

4 If you work for an executive who frequently makes changes to her/his dictation, have a wide margin in which to record the alterations clearly.

5 Always date each page of dictation in the right-hand corner. It aids retrieval of work.

6 Draw a line across the page after each item of dictation.

7 Place an elastic band around the pages already written on and transcribed. This will enable you to find your place quickly.

8 Make sure you have plenty of space in which to work.

9 If you miss a word or cannot keep up with the speed of dictation, say so, at an appropriate point.

10 Under normal circumstances do not interrupt the executive whilst s/he is dictating.

When dictation is completed you should transcribe it as quickly and as accurately as possible. Whether the style is fully blocked (see Unit 5) with open or closed punctuation (see Unit 6, Element 6.1) will depend on the house style of your company.

Make sure you keep up to date with what is happening in the company. Remember that a good knowledge of a company's business will aid correct transcription rather than something which is complete nonsense.

**FACT
FINDER**

Transcribing dictation

1 When transcribing make sure that any item which is urgent or needs special attention is dealt with immediately.

2 Be watchful of any corrections or special instructions made during dictation.

3 Consult a dictionary if there is any doubt about the spelling of a word.

4 Never forget the impact of good display.

5 Always put a straight line through notes transcribed. This should ensure that no item is left untranscribed.

6 Always pay particular attention to proof-reading your work before handing it to your executive for signature.

7 Keep used notebooks and file them in case of any query in the future.